# *more* POPULAR ANTIQUES *and their* VALUES

Compiled and Edited by

TONY CURTIS

1st Edition April 1973
2nd Impression April 1974

2nd Edition July 1974 (revised prices)
2nd Impression July 1975

3rd Edition April 1977 (revised prices)
2nd Impression September 1977
3rd Impression February 1978
4th Impression March 1979

4th Edition May 1979 (revised prices)

**LYLE PUBLICATIONS LIMITED**

**GLENMAYNE    GALASHIELS    SELKIRKSHIRE    SCOTLAND**

# CONTENTS

# INTRODUCTION

Following the enormous success of Popular Antiques and their Values, I have compiled this completely new companion edition.

The items chosen are, on the whole, representative of the middle section of the market with the addition of a few rare pieces, which, although not to be found in every corner shop, command such surprisingly high prices as to make their inclusion of benefit to the reader.

I have avoided wherever possible the kind of definitive description so beloved of antique 'exports' which relate to those 'classic' pieces which are rarely to be seen in any but the most exclusively expensive salerooms. Instead, I have given the essentail details and a value calculated from auctions and retail outlets, which is the price I believe a dealer should pay for goods in fair condition.

As regards values of individual pieces, these vary considerably from place to place and are dependent to a great extent on the localised variations in fashionable taste. It is this local variation which accounts for the wide ranging activities of professional antique dealers and makes generalised pricing somewhat difficult.

It will, however, give a fair idea of the value which I hope will be of assistance to those who, while having an appreciation of the look and feel of antiques, lack the confidence to plunge in at the deep end.

When valuing antiques, the condition is of prime importance, for it often costs as much as the original price paid to put an object in a saleable condition, and this must be taken into account when calculations are made.

Beyond its purely aesthetic appeal, articles of a bygone age frequently have one great advantage over that which is produced at the present time: it generally appreciates in value as each year passes and few people in this day and age would disagree with the proposition that beautiful pieces whose investment potential may be as high as that of property is an asset indeed.

TONY CURTIS

S.B.N. 0-902921-62-2

Printed in Great Britain by

APOLLO PRESS    DOMINION WAY    WORTHING    SUSSEX

# MONARCHS

| | |
|---|---|
| HENRY IV | 1399 - 1413 |
| HENRY V | 1413 - 1422 |
| HENRY VI | 1422 - 1461 |
| EDWARD IV | 1461 - 1483 |
| EDWARD V | 1483 - 1483 |
| RICHARD III | 1483 - 1485 |
| HENRY VII | 1485 - 1509 |
| HENRY VIII | 1509 - 1547 |
| EDWARD VI | 1547 - 1553 |
| MARY | 1553 - 1558 |
| ELIZABETH | 1558 - 1603 |
| JAMES I | 1603 - 1625 |
| CHARLES I | 1625 - 1649 |
| COMMONWEALTH | 1649 - 1660 |
| CHARLES II | 1660 - 1685 |
| JAMES II | 1685 - 1689 |
| WILLIAM & MARY | 1689 - 1695 |
| WILLIAM III | 1695 - 1702 |
| ANNE | 1702 - 1714 |
| GEORGE I | 1714 - 1727 |
| GEORGE II | 1727 - 1760 |
| GEORGE III | 1760 - 1820 |
| GEORGE IV | 1820 - 1830 |
| WILLIAM IV | 1830 - 1837 |
| VICTORIA | 1837 - 1901 |
| EDWARD VII | 1901 - 1910 |

# PERIODS

| | |
|---|---|
| TUDOR PERIOD | 1485 - 1603 |
| ELIZABETHAN PERIOD | 1558 - 1603 |
| INIGO JONES | 1572 - 1652 |
| JACOBEAN PERIOD | 1603 - 1688 |
| STUART PERIOD | 1603 - 1714 |
| A. C. BOULLE | 1642 - 1732 |
| LOUIS X1V PERIOD | 1643 - 1715 |
| GRINLING GIBBONS | 1648 - 1726 |
| CROMWELLIAN PERIOD | 1649 - 1660 |
| CAROLEAN PERIOD | 1660 - 1685 |
| WILLIAM KENT | 1684 - 1748 |
| WILLIAM & MARY PERIOD | 1689 - 1702 |
| QUEEN ANNE PERIOD | 1702 - 1714 |
| GEORGIAN PERIOD | 1714 - 1820 |
| T. CHIPPENDALE | 1715 - 1762 |
| LOUIS XV PERIOD | 1723 - 1774 |
| A. HEPPLEWHITE | 1727 - 1788 |
| ADAM PERIOD | 1728 - 1792 |
| ANGELICA KAUFMANN | 1741 - 1807 |
| T. SHERATON | 1751 - 1806 |
| LOUIS XV1 | 1774 - 1793 |
| T. SHEARER | (circa) 1780 |
| REGENCY PERIOD | 1800 - 1830 |
| EMPIRE PERIOD | 1804 - 1815 |
| VICTORIAN PERIOD | 1830 - 1901 |
| EDWARDIAN PERIOD | 1901 - 1910 |

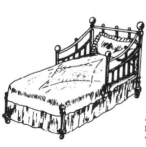

An extremely fine inlaid mahogany Edwardian bed with painted panels, 4ft wide. **$190 £95**

Victorian child's brass bed. **$180 £90**

Early 19th century Empire style bed with ormolu enrichments. **$650 £325**

Late 18th century mahogany four poster bed, 53ins wide. **$800 £400**

Victorian brass bed, 4ft 6ins wide. **$400 £200**

17th century oak four poster bed, 5ft. wide, 7ft. 3in. long. **$8,000 £4,000**

Magnificent 19th century carved rosewood four poster bed. **$3,000 £1,500**

Superb Victorian brass bed with original drapes. **$950 £475**

Early 19th century boulle bed with fine ormolu mounts. **$4,600 £2,300**

**11**

# BOOKCASES SMALL

Small Edwardian inlaid mahogany open fronted set of two shelves with a compartment enclosed by a leaded glass door. $40 £20

Finely carved Victorian open fronted bookcase with adjustable shelves, 6ft 6 ins wide. $350 £175

Edwardian mahogany three tier revolving bookstand. $160 £80

A set of Regency mahogany shelves. $140 £70

Early 19th century ebony and amboyna wood breakfront bookcase. 5ft 6ins wide. $800 £400

Regency period rosewood open bookcase with a fall front secretaire drawer with a satinwood interior. $1,100 £550

Exquisite small bookcase, circa 1800, with floral enrichment, 10½ins x. 47ins x 19½ins. $450 £225

Late George III breakfront bookcase in simulated rosewood and gilt, 61 ins long. $840 £420

Fine quality George III mahogany open bookshelves. $1,320 £660

Early 19th century
pine breakfront book-
case, 6ft wide. $1,900 £950

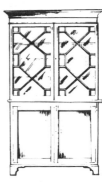

Victorian mahogany
bookcase with three
enclosed shelves, drawer
and cupboard. $200 £100

Georgian mahogany
bookcase with astragal
glazed doors to the upper
section and inlaid
panelled doors below,
with bracket feet, 4ft
wide. $480 £240

Regency period rosewood
breakfront bookcase
with the original grilles.
$2,200 £1,100

Late 18th century
figured mahogany
breakfront bookcase
with adjustable doors
and panelled cupboard
doors. $2,300 £1,150

Sheraton mahogany
breakfront bookcase
circa 1780, 8ft 6 ins
high, 6ft 7ins long.
$3,600 £1,800

George III bookcase
in finely grained mahogany
with astragal glazed
doors. $900 £450

Chippendale period
mahogany breakfront
bookcase with a carved
cornice and fluted pil-
asters, 8ft 9ins wide.
$8,000 £4,000

Hepplewhite bookcase
with crossbanded
and panelled doors.
$1,800 £900    13

# BUREAU BOOKCASES

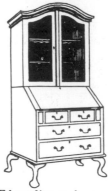

Edwardian oak bureau bookcase, 3ft wide.
**$140 £70**

Edwardian mahogany domed top bureau bookcase on cabriole leg supports. **$300 £150**

An exceptionally fine quality inlaid mahogany bureau bookcase 3ft 2ins wide. **$1,050 £525**

A fine quality mahogany bureau bookcase inlaid with floral garlands.
**$1,080 £540**

19th century rosewood cylinder top bureau with pull-out writing board and bookcase above.
**$480 £240**

A fine George III mahogany bookcase.
**$1,740 £870**

Late 18th century Dutch marquetry bureau bookcase the domed cornice carved with floral and foliate scrolls. **$5,000 £2,500**

Sheraton harewood cylinder desk and bookcase with a tambour front, 6ft high.
**$5,500 £2,750**

A fine quality Queen Anne walnut bureau bookcase only 26ins wide, 79ins high.
**$9,600 £4,800**

Early 20th century oak bureau on a stretcher base, 2ft 9ins wide. $100 £50

19th century inlaid mahogany roll top desk, 3ft 3ins wide. $600 £300

19th century French rosewood and marquetry bureau with a pierced brass gallery and cabriole legs. $480 £240

Small 18th century oak bureau only 2ft 7ins wide. $650 £325

A small early 19th century mahogany bureau decorated with bows, ribbons and garlands of flowers, 2ft 2ins wide. $560 £280

Mid 18th century fruitwood bureau of a good golden brown colour, 36ins wide, 39ins high, 19ins deep. $1,200 £600

Edwardian inlaid mahogany bureau on splayed feet, 2ft. 6in. wide. $240 £120

17th century oak desk on turned supports with stretchers. $1,000 £500

A magnificent quality Dutch marquetry bureau 3ft 5ins wide. $3,740 £1,870

# CABINETS

A fine Victorian burr walnut dwarf cabinet. **$540 £270**

A Regency ebonised cabinet with brass string inlay and a figured marble top. **$420 £210**

19th century Dutch marquetry cabinet. **$840 £420**

An unusual mahogany collector's cabinet with assorted sized oak lined drawers numbered one to nine, 24ins wide, circa 1790. **$450 £225**

A rare padouk wood cabinet with superbly carved 'sunburst' panels, 47ins wide, 76ins high, circa 1770. **$1,100 £525**

English Regency cabinet on stand with black japan and chinoiserie decoration. **$1,800 £900**

A gilt lacquer and shibayama work cabinet. **$2,400 £1,200**

A superb porcelain mounted ebony cabinet with Meissen plaques depicting romantic scenes and court portraits **$14,400 £7,200**

Late 18th century side cabinet veneered with satinwood. **$6,000 £3,000**

William IV mahogany music canterbury.
**$320 £160**

Victorian walnut music canterbury fitted with a drawer, 23ins wide.
**$200 £100**

A fine Victorian ebonised canterbury. **$140 £70**

A fine Regency rosewood music canterbury.
**$340 £170**

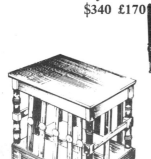

Early 19th century mahogany music canterbury **$290 £145**

An unusual Regency canterbury in rosewood.
**$360 £180**

Regency rosewood canterbury with an unusual lidded top, 19ins x 15ins, circa 1820. **$500 £250**

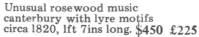

An exceptionally fine quality Sheraton satinwood canterbury. **$2,000 £1,000**

Unusual rosewood music canterbury with lyre motifs circa 1820, 1ft 7ins long. **$450 £225**

# DINING CHAIRS

Edwardian mahogany
dining chair on turned
legs.
Set of 4  $110  £55
Set of 6  $200  £100

Late Victorian Queen
Anne style beechwood
dining chair.
Set of 4  $110  £55
Set of 6  $200  £100

Edwardian inlaid
mahogany
dining chair.
Set of 4  $260  £130
Set of 6  $400  £200

Victorian bentwood
dining chair.
Set of 4  $90  £45
Set of 6  $150  £75

Victorian cabriole
leg dining chair in
walnut.
Set of 4  $360  £180
Set of 6  $800  £400

Victorian mahogany
dining chair on
turned legs.
Set of 4  $220  £110
Set of 6  $380  £190

William IV turned
leg mahogany
dining chair.
Set of 4  $240  £120
Set of 6  $430  £215

Late Regency
mahogany
dining chair on
turned legs.
Set of 4  $340  £170
Set of 6  $720  £360

Regency sabre leg
dining chair in
rosewood.
Set of 4  $500  £250
Set of 6  $960  £480

Hepplewhite
period shield
back dining
chair.
Set of 4  $480  £240
Set of 6  $960  £480

Chippendale
period mahogany
dining chair.
Set of 4  $580  £290
Set of 6  $1,080  £540

18th century elm
ladderback chair
with rush seat.
Set of 4  $290  £145
Set of 6  $500  £250

Mid-19th century
bentwood rocking
chair with a cane seat
and back. **$190 £95**

Edwardian mahogany
open sided armchair
with a pierced splat
and cabriole legs. **$60 £30**

Victorian mahogany
chair-steps. **$60 £30**

Edwardian inlaid
mahogany armchair.
**$100 £50**

Regency mahogany
sabre leg armchair.
**$180 £90**

Chippendale period
ladderback armchair.
**$280 £140**

Victorian scroll
arm chair on
turned legs. **$80 £40**

Good quality late 18th
century Hepplewhite
japanned armchair with
a cane seat. **$420 £210**

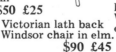

Victorian Elizabethan
style oak armchair. **$50 £25**

Victorian lath back
Windsor chair in elm.
**$90 £45**

18th century yew wood
Windsor chair of good
colour and condition.
**$300 £150**

17th century oak
elbow chair.
**$800 £400**

19

# EASY CHAIRS

Edwardian ebonised armchair on short cabriole legs. $84 £42

Nicely shaped Victorian iron frame ladies chair on turned legs with brass cup castors. $190 £95

Victorian turned leg grandfather chair in walnut. $240 £120

Victorian cabriole leg occasional chair in mahogany covered in moss green velvet. $270 £135

Good quality finely carved rosewood Victorian grandfather chair with cabriole legs. $350 £175

William IV mahogany armchair covered in tan leather. $290 £145

A good Louis XV period carved giltwood Bergere, circa 1760. $920 £460

A fine quality George II library chair. $4,000 £2,000

Fine period wing chair, circa 1790. $720 £360

An Edwardian walnut chest of drawers.
**$40 £20**

Mid 19th century mahogany chest of three long and two short graduated drawers, on splay feet. **$150 £75**

Victorian mahogany bow front chest of three long and two short graduated cock headed drawers, 3ft 6ins wide. **$150 £75**

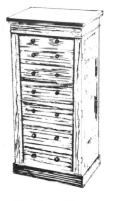

Good quality Victorian rosewood Wellington chest of seven drawers, 2ft wide. **$300 £150**

George II bow front chest of drawers, 2ft 11½ins wide.
**$720 £360**

George I chest of Cuban mahogany on bracket feet, with brass carrying handles. **$680 £340**

Early 18th century oyster veneered walnut chest of drawers on bun feet. **$1,100 £550**

George I walnut and yew wood parquetry chest inlaid with satinwood, 39in. wide. **$1,300 £650**

Fine Charles II chest with bone and ebony inlay, circa 1670.
**$1,400 £700**

21

## CHESTS ON CHESTS

George III mahogany tallboy with oak lined drawers, circa 1820, 41ins wide.

**$450 £225**

Late l8th century mahogany tallboy with brass loop handles and bracket feet. 3ft 6ins wide. **$550 £275**

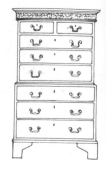

George III mahogany tallboy with a fretwork frieze. **$590 £295**

A fine mahogany bow fronted chest on chest with a shaped apron and splayed feet. £375
**$1,250 £625**

Continental red walnut chest on stand with basket weave carving.
**$1,200 £600**

Late l8th century mahogany chest on chest with a secretaire drawer, elaborate cornice and ogee feet. **$2,400 £1,200**

Late l7th century oak chest on stand in fine original condition.
**$1,200 £600**

A fine quality Queen Anne walnut chest on chest of good colour.
**$2,500 £1,250**

A fine Charles II walnut chest on stand with seaweed marquetry decoration, circa 1686.
**$2,860 £1,430**

Late Victorian mahogany chiffonier, 3ft 3ins wide .
**$70 £35**

Early Victorian mahogany chiffonier. **$220 £110**

Early 19th century japanned chiffonier decorated with motifs en grisaille. 31ins wide. **$440 £220**

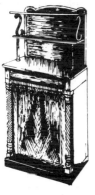

Small early 19th century mahogany chiffonier, 24ins wide, 54ins high. **$360 £180**

Early 19th century breakfront chiffonier in rosewood.
**$1,250 £625**

An attractive and finely figured mahogany chiffonier only 2ft 2½ins wide, 4ft 1ins high. **$650 £325**

Early 19th century mahogany chiffonier with a fall front secretaire drawer. **$960 £480**

A superb Georgian mahogany chiffonier inlaid with brass. 25ins wide. **$1,560 £780**

Early 19th century mahogany chiffonier with a fitted writing drawer. **$1,050 £525**

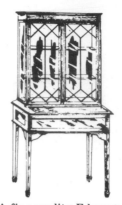

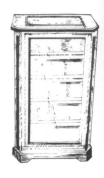

19th century heart shaped specimen table in satinwood with floral marquetry decoration. **$500 £250**

A fine quality Edwardian inlaid mahogany display cabinet with astragal glazed doors. **$600 £300**

A good quality Edwardian inlaid burr walnut music cabinet. **$90 £45**

Edwardian mahogany corner display cabinet inlaid with boxwood. **$355 £175**

Edwardian inlaid mahogany china cabinet, 4ft 6ins wide. **$400 £200**

Heavily carved Oriental hardwood display cabinet from the 19th century. **$550 £275**

19th century satinwood display cabinet decorated in the Sheraton manner, 48in. wide. **$1,800 £900**

A superb French rosewood vitrine with Vernis Martin panels. **$4,000 £2,000**

19th century French vitrine in rosewood with inlaid flowers, 3ft. wide x 6ft. high **$1,200 £600**

Edwardian mahogany
bedside cupboard.
**$20 £10**

George III mahogany
bedroom steps with a
pot cupboard and bidet
drawer.   **$250 £125**

A good Victorian
mahogany pot cupboard
with a figured marble
top.   **$80 £40**

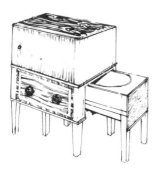

Late 18th century
satinwood bedside
table.  **$850 £425**

A fine early 19th century
travelling commode with
a spode basin and brass
fittings.   **$300 £150**

George III mahogany
tray top commode with
drawer and cupboard.
**$180 £90**

George III mahogany
bedside cupboard.
**$120 £60**

A mahogany inlaid bow
front commode with
hinged top and front of
simulated drawers, 2ft.
1in. wide.   **$90 £45**

Early 19th century
mahogany pot
cupboard on fine
turned legs. **$84 £42**

## COMMODE CHESTS

19th century Louis XV style ormolu mounted, marble top bombe commode. $660 £330

Louis XV marquetry and kingwood commode 4ft 6ins wide.
$1,500 £750

Louis XVI walnut commode with a frieze drawer and three long drawers below, with a figured marble top.
$1,400 £700

18th century Dutch commode in rosewood, 4ft wide. $2,400 £1,200

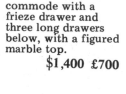

Louis XV ormolu mounted kingwood commode signed Migeon, 52ins wide.
$9,600 £4,800

A fine quality Georgian figured mahogany commode with a fitted top drawer containing a mirror and assorted compartments.
$2,000 £1,000

18th century Venetian two drawer commode painted with flowers on a green ground, 1.12 metres wide.
$7,700 £3,850

Small Adam style serpentine commode in satinwood, circa 1785, 50ins wide. $11,000 £5,500

18th century two door commode in the style of John Cobb.
$16,800 £8,400

George III mahogany
corner cupboard with
shaped shelves.
**$200 £100**

Late 18th century
mahogany hanging
corner cupboard.
**$240 £120**

A fine quality Sheraton
corner cupboard of
rich chestnut colour,
57ins high, circa 1785.
**$480 £240**

Louis Philippe corner
display shelves with
pierced brass galleries
and a white marble
top.      **$360 £180**

A good 18th century
stripped pine corner
cupboard with three
shelves and a dentil
cornice.  **$450 £225**

Victorian burr walnut
corner cabinet with
ormolu mounts. **$560
£280**

Edwardian inlaid
rosewood corner
cabinet with a
multitude of galleries
and mirrors.
**$400 £200**

George III corner
cupboard in beautifully
figured mahogany.
**$660 £330**

An excellent 18th century
walnut and marquetry
corner cupboard.
**$2,200 £1,100**

Late 17th century English oak court cupboard.
**$830 £415**

A late 17th century oak tridarn, 53in. wide.
**$1,800 £900**

17th century oak court cupboard. **$1,450 £725**

Oak duodarn with carved borders and pilasters, 1.75cm. high. **$1,050 £525**

Small buffet in honey coloured oak, magnificently carved, with panels and door inlaid in various woods, circa 1765.
4ft 8ins long, 2ft deep, 4ft 4ins high. **$1,700 £850**

Jacobean oak court cupboard of good colour, 82in. high.
**$1,200 £600**

Charles II oak buffet, 39½ins wide.
**$2,200 £1,100**

A fine quality early 17th century oak livery cupboard. **$2,400 £1,200**

A fine James I oak court cupboard.
**$3,000 £1,500**

Victorian ebonised credenza with glazed ends and a panelled cupboard centre door with gilt decoration.
**$400  £200**

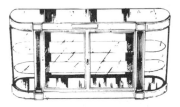

Victorian ebonised credenza with ivory and ormolu decoration, a mirror back and glass shelves, 6ft 6ins wide.     **$400  £200**

Small Victorian inlaid walnut breakfront credenza with ormolu decoration.     **$900  £450**

Victorian breakfront burr walnut credenza with marquetry decoration and fine ormolu mounts. **$950  £475**

19th century burr walnut credenza with bowed glass ends and a panelled centre door with inlaid decoration, ormolu mounts and banding.     **$900  £450**

Victorian walnut inlaid, banded and marquetry serpentine fronted cabinet of French design, 5ft. 3in. wide.
**$1,400  £700**

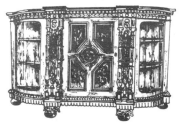

19th century Italian gilded credenza with gesso ornamentation and a shaped marble top.   **$1,500  £750**

19th century walnut and rosewood credenza with ormolu mounts, 6ft 1ins long, 3ft 5ins high.
**$2,000  £1,000**

# CUPBOARDS

A mid 17th century oak buffet, 5ft wide.
**$1,000 £500**

Flemish oak cupboard of good colour and condition.
**$850 £425**

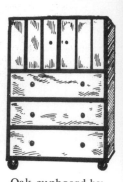

Oak cupboard by Heal and Sons, circa 1905.
**$305 £150**

16th century German oak sacristy cupboard.
**$850 £425**

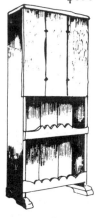

17th century Spanish cupboard, 29ins wide. **$800 £400**

A fine 17th century carved oak cupboard. **$1,200 £600**

A fine 18th century oak cabinet of good colour.
**$1,750 £875**

Rare George II portable cupboard in mahogany, 6ft 5ins tall, 13ins deep.
**$1,200 £600**

English 16th century oak cupboard, 5ft 7½ins wide.
**$6,000 £3,000**

Mid 19th century walnut davenport. **$350 £175**

A Victorian rosewood davenport with a satinwood interior. **$500 £250**

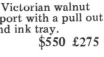

Early Victorian walnut davenport with a pull out pen and ink tray.
**$550 £275**

A fine quality 19th century rosewood davenport with a cupboard door concealing four drawers. **$550 £275**

Early Victorian satinwood davenport with rosewood banding. **$650 £325**

An unusual Gothic style 19th century davenport. **$700 £350**

Mid 19th century burr walnut davenport with cabriole leg front supports. **$1,050 £525**

Fine quality early Victorian walnut piano top davenport with gilt decoration
**$1,200 £600**

A small George III davenport in finely figured mahogany with rosewood cross-banding, circa 1795, 15ins wide.
**$1,300 £650**

# DRESSERS

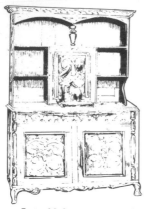

Late 19th century oak dresser with carved cupboard doors, 4ft 8ins wide. $240 £120

Early Victorian pine dresser with a nicely shaped frieze and apron. $340 £170

Georgian oak dresser with cabriole legs and three drawers. $1,500 £750

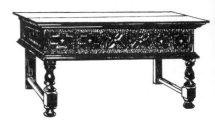

Early 18th century oak dresser with back board. $850 £425

Late 17th century oak dresser with geometric mouldings. $1,500 £750

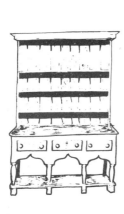

Early 18th century oak dresser, 5ft 4ins wide. $1,200 £600

A good quality late 18th century oak dresser with centre panelled cupboard doors and nine drawers. $1,600 £800

Rustic 18th century pine dresser with primitive silhouette legs to the base, two drawers and a pewter plate rack, 6lins wide. $800 £400

Late 18th century
mahogany folding
top dressing table.
$400 £200

Late Victorian walnut
dressing table. $90 £45

Georgian mahogany
serpentine front
dressing chest with
a fitted top drawer.
$1,400 £700

George III kneehole
dressing table, 41 in.
wide. $250 £125

Fine quality
Georgian mahogany
dressing and
writing table, 36ins
wide, 23ins deep,
31 ins high. $2,400 £1,200

Small late 18th century
bow fronted mahogany
dressing table. $500 £250

Late Victorian
mahogany shaving
stand with boxwood
string inlay. $70 £35

Late 18th century
mahogany chest with
a fitted top drawer.
$700 £350

Victorian mahogany
shaving stand with an
adjustable mirror.
$80 £40

Early 19th century two tier dumb waiter on a tripod base with brass castors.  $600 £300

William IV mahogany dumb waiter, 42ins high.  $400 £200

George III mahogany dumb waiter on a tripod base with pad feet.  $480 £240

Late 18th century mahogany three tier dumb waiter.  $450 £225

A good George III three tier mahogany dumb waiter on a tripod base with ball and claw feet.  $1,200 £600

George III mahogany dumb waiter, circa 1790 .  $500 £250

George III mahogany four tier dumb waiter of faded colour, circa 1790.  $550 £275

Regency mahogany dumb waiter on tripod stand.  $1,150 £575

Early 19th century mahogany dumb waiter, 5ft high.  $480 £240

Victorian mahogany
secretaire with a fall
front revealing a
cupboard and
numerous drawers.
**$360 £180**

A good walnut
escritoire with a
well fitted interior
32ins wide, circa 1840. **$530
£265**

A fine 19th century
Dutch marquetry
escritoire.
**$1,500 £750**

Mid 19th century
French ebonised
bonheur du jour.
**$350 £175**

19th century kingwood
and rosewood escritoire
with serpentine front
and sides, 25½ins wide,
49ins high.
**$1,500 £750**

A good quality 19th
century marquetry
escritoire with ormolu
mounts. **$1,600 £800**

William and Mary walnut
escritoire on stand.
**$1,700 £850**

William and Mary escritoire
decorated with floral
marquetry 3ft 4ins wide.
**$2,400 £1,200**

A William and Mary period
double domed escritoire
in walnut. **$3,000 £1,500**

# LOWBOYS

Mid 18th century country made oak lowboy.
**$270 £135**

18th century oak lowboy on square legs chamfered on the inside edge.
**$260 £130**

Georgian oak lowboy crossbanded with mahogany. **$320 £160**

George I fruitwood dressing table on tapering legs with pad feet. **$480 £240**

Mahogany lowboy on square legs, circa 1780. **$540 £270**

Late 18th century mahogany lowboy 35ins wide.
**$480 £240**

Queen Anne lowboy in oak with cabriole legs and pear drop handles. **$540 £270**

Late 17th century oak lowboy crossbanded in walnut. **$600 £300**

George I lowboy, on cabriole legs, 32in. wide, 19½in. deep, 19in. high, circa 1720.
**$950 £475**

Victorian mahogany seaman's chest with sunken wooden handles. **$340 £170**

Regency mahogany military chest with sunken wooden knobs and brass straps. 3ft 3ins wide.**$400 £200**

Two-part military chest, full brass bound with iron carrying handles, circa 1850, 42in. long x 18in. deep x 42in. high. **$550 £275**

Early 19th century camphorwood military chest with canted corners and a secretaire fitment. **$800 £400**

Captain's rare secretaire chest from China, ivory inlays, circa 1850, rich walnut colour.**$920 £460**

Early 19th century mahogany military chest with a secretaire in the centre drawer. **$750 £275**

Regency mahogany secretaire military chest with fold down bookshelves above, circa 1820. 39ins wide. **$840 £420**

An unusually small secretaire military chest only 30ins wide. **$860 £430**

An exceptionally fine teak secretaire military chest, only 30ins wide, circa 1820.**$1,100 £550**

## PEDESTAL & KNEEHOLE DESKS

Late 19th century oak pedestal desk, the tambour shutter concealing drawers and pigeon holes.
$240 £120

Late 19th century mahogany pedestal writing desk on a platform base, 4ft 6ins wide.
$300 £150

19th century Sheraton style kneehole desk inlaid with satinwood shell and fan designs.
$800 £400

·Good quality 19th century. red boulle pedestal desk with fine ormolu mounts.
$1,800 £900

A George III mahogany architects kneehole desk with an adjustable top. 3ft 2ins wide. $1,300 £650

An unusual 18th century walnut kneehole desk.
$2,000 £1,000

A good George II kneehole desk with a flush top and bracket feet. $1,450 £725

A small 19th century marquetry kneehole desk decorated with flowers and floral sprays.
$1,900 £950

Small George III figured mahogany kneehole desk with writing slide and brass drop handles.
$1,650 £825

Edwardian mahogany and satinwood banded two tier plant stand. **$40 £20**

A fine early 19th century Regency gilt and gesso torchere. **$360 £180**

Early 19th century mahogany knife urn and pedestal with cupboard door. **$550 £275**

Edwardian mahogany jardiniere stand. **$80 £40**

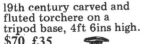

Regency period green marble pillar with ormolu mounts. **$340 £170**

Early 18th century walnut torchere 3ft 8ins high. **$420 £210**

19th century carved and fluted torchere on a tripod base, 4ft 6ins high. **$70 £35**

A 19th century kingwood and marquetry plinth with ormolu mounts and a marble top. **$540 £270**

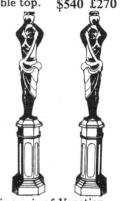

Pair of finely carved Regency walnut torcheres with simulated malachite and marble bases. **$2,000 £1,000**

Pair of Regency period blackamoor figures, 98cm. high. **$2,200 £1,100**

A fine pair of Venetian Blackamoor figures 6ft 6ins high, circa 1820. **$2,600 £1,300**

# SECRETAIRES

Late 18th century mahogany bow fronted secretaire. **$720 £360**

Early 19th century, Sheraton style secretaire with a satinwood interior and hide liner. **$620 £310**

An attractive well figured mahogany secretaire, the writing drawer with satinwood drawers and cupboard, 42ins wide, circa 1820. **$600 £300**

Secretaire cabinet in walnut made by P. Waals. **$3,000 £1,500**

Late 18th century English mahogany secretaire inlaid with stained and engraved fruitwoods. **$12,000 £6,000**

Regency breakfront cabinet in mahogany with a secretaire drawer, 54ins wide, circa 1825. **$1,200 £600**

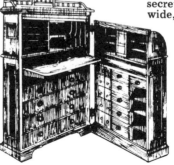

Early 19th century writing cabinet with drawers and graduated shelves, 35ins wide, 71ins high. **$1,000 £500**

19th century North American oak office desk, 4ft 9ins wide, circa 1880. **$900 £450**

Early 19th century coromandel wood cabinet with a secretaire drawer. **$950 £475**

Victorian mahogany secretaire bookcase of three adjustable shelves enclosed by two glazed doors. 3ft 6 ins wide. **$260 £130**

A good quality Regency mahogany secretaire bookcase 3ft 7ins wide. **$900 £450**

Late 18th century inlaid mahogany secretaire bookcase 4ft wide, with a nicely fitted interior. **$1,050 £525**

Regency period secretaire bookcase in mahogany 3ft 3 ins wide, 7ft 6ins high, circa 1815. **$1,260 £630**

Late Georgian mahogany secretaire bookcase of fine quality with a satinwood fitted drawer, 44ins wide. **$780 £390**

An attractive mahogany secretaire bookcase, circa 1825, 32ins wide, 7ft 3ins high, 19ins deep. **$1,380 £690**

Good quality Hepplewhite secretaire bookcase with Gothic formations in the glazed door. **$2,160 £1,080**

Regency rosewood secretaire bookcase inlaid with brass and ornamented with gilt metal marbled columns. **$1,320 £660**

A fine English secretaire cabinet circa 1780 veneered with sycamore and decorated with rosewood **$8,000 £4,000**

41

An attractive simulated rosewood couch of the Regency period with ormolu mounts.
$600 £300

Edwardian pale mahogany open sided settee on cabriole leg supports. $200 £100

Early Victorian walnut couch on cabriole legs.
$450 £225

Late l8th century mahogany settee 7ft 5ins long.          $800 £400

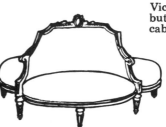

Victorian walnut framed sofa with ormolu mounts.          $960 £480

Victorian walnut framed button back settee on cabriole legs. $820 £410

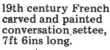

19th century French carved and painted conversation settee, 7ft 6ins long.
$1,380 £690

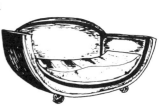

Ebonised Empire style chaise longue with painted decoration.
$770 £385

A gondola sofa by Marcel Coard.
$28,000 £14,000

Late 19th century mahogany open sided three piece suite on fine turned legs terminating in brass castors.   $260 £130

Late 19th century inlaid mahogany three piece suite on square tapering legs.                                    $400 £200

Early Victorian three piece walnut suite on cabriole legs:
$1,500 £750

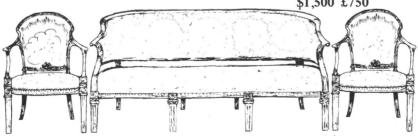

A good quality Louis XVI three seat settee and four armchairs.                                    $2,860 £1,430

# SIDEBOARDS

Victorian mahogany pedestal sideboard with four drawers and two cupboards. **$300 £150**

Mid Victorian mahogany pedestal sideboard with a mirror back in a carved frame. **$250 £125**

Edwardian carved mahogany sideboard with a bevelled mirror back, two drawers and two cupboards. **$100 £50**

Early 19th century mahogany breakfront sideboard on turned legs with a recessed tambour in the centre. **$800 £400**

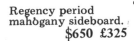

Late 18th century Sheraton style mahogany sideboard 60ins long. **$1,000 £500**

Regency period mahogany sideboard. **$650 £325**

A good quality Sheraton mahogany serpentine front sideboard, 5ft wide. **$1,300 £650**

Small George III mahogany sideboard in excellent condition, on tapered legs with spade feet, circa 1790. **$1,200 £600**

Sheraton period mahogany sideboard 70ins wide. **£750** **$2,000 £1,000**

Late Victorian footstool on bun feet. **$14 £7**

Edwardian inlaid mahogany piano stool, 1ft 9ins wide. **$60 £30**

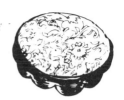

19th century walnut footstool with a beadwork cover. **$24 £12**

Victorian mahogany revolving piano stool. **$60 £30**

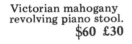

Early Victorian mahogany dressing table stool on cabriole legs, 1ft 10ins wide. **$110 £55**

Good Victorian rosewood revolving piano stool. **$70 £35**

Good quality Regency period 'X' frame stool. **$230 £115**

17th century oak joint stool. **$580 £290**

Louis XV cream painted and gilt decorated window seats. **$1,200 £600**

Edwardian folding top
card table in walnut.
$125 £65

Edwardian mahogany
envelope card table with
a drawer.    $195 £100

Victorian folding top
card table in rosewood
on a platform base with
bun feet.    $280 £140

Early 19th century
mahogany card table
inlaid with satinwood
on fluted legs.$350 £175

Regency period
rosewood card table
with splay feet.$550 £275

Victorian inlaid
burr walnut
folding-top card
table on a stretcher
base.    $260 £130

Georgian satinwood
card table painted
with garlands of
flowers. $1,150 £575

George I carved walnut
games table crossbanded
and feather strung, 86cm.
wide.    $1,900 £950

George II folding
top mahogany card
table with projecting
corners, carved
cabriole legs and
scroll feet. $1,200 £600

19th century gilt consol table with a shaped green marble top. $450 £225

A small mid 18th century giltwood consol table with a figured marble top, 25ins wide. $780 £390

19th century boulle consol table with ormolu mounts. $1,050 £525

A fine French Regency giltwood consol table 6ft 5ins wide. $4,620 £2,310

18th century gilt consol table with a fine carved eagle support. $2,340 £1,200

18th century gilt consol table attributed to Thomas Johnson. $10,000 £5,000

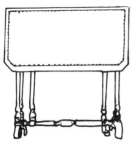

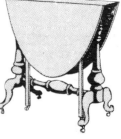

Mahogany, inlaid and satinwood banded, Sutherland tea table on turned legs, 2ft. wide. $155 £80

An early Victorian rosewood Sutherland table on barley twist supports, 3ft 3ins x 6ins top when closed. $215 £110

Early Victorian burr walnut Sutherland table on cabriole leg supports. $290 £150

19th century walnut
pedestal table inlaid
with boxwood, 35ins
wide. **$430 £220**

Round Victorian
mahogany dining
table on a tripod
base. **$300 £150**

Well figured and original
mid 19th century walnut
tilt top table, 4ft.6in.
wide. **$650 £325**

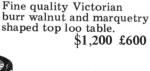

A good Regency table
in burr walnut cross-
banded with rosewood,
42ins diameter.
**$1,000 £500**

William IV mahogany
centre table with a good
quality shaped platform
base and elaborate lions
paw feet. **$700 £350**

Fine quality Victorian
burr walnut and marquetry
shaped top loo table.
**$1,200 £600**

Regency mahogany
breakfast table cross-
banded with kingwood,
circa 1820. **$1,200 £600**

A fine quality Regency
period rosewood
library table. **$2,340 £1,200**

A fine Regency
circular breakfast
table in burr maple
inlaid with rose-
wood, 4ft 1½ins
diameter.
**$2,435 $1,250**

Georgian mahogany two flap table with oval leaves and pad feet. $500 £250

Late 18th century mahogany drop leaf table on six legs with ball and claw feet. $480 £240

Late 18th century oak drop leaf cottage dining table. $165 £85

Late 19th century oak gateleg table with barley twist supports. $95 £50

Queen Anne oak gateleg of rich faded colour. $950 £475

Small 17th century oak gateleg table. $850 £425

17th century oak gateleg table with square flaps and a double gate action. $1,200 £600

A fine quality Charles I gateleg table. $2,000 £1,000

An extremely fine large Irish wakes table in mahogany, from the mid 18th century. $2,925 £1,500

19th century red boulle centre table
with cabriole legs and ormolu mounts.
$1,500  £750

Mahogany two flap dining table on
six square tapered legs, circa 1820.
$485  £250

George III mahogany wakes table. $1,460  £750

Regency period extending dining table
in mahogany with an unusual split
pedestal action.      $1,655  £850

18th century oak table, 72in. wide.
$1,747  £900

George III three pedestal table in
mahogany 10ft 5ins long. $2,040  £1,020

Elizabeth I oak refectory table with
ground level stretchers, 10ft long.
$6,000  £3,000

A massive early Georgian oak
refectory table on six turned legs,
with a plank top and drawer at either
end, 28ft 8ins long.   $8,775  £4,500

19th century mahogany Pembroke table on turned legs, 2ft 9ins wide when open. **$120 £60**

George III mahogany Pembroke table on square tapering legs. **$195 £100**

Regency period mahogany Pembroke table with satinwood crossbanding, 2ft 3ins wide when closed. **$300 £150**

Sheraton satinwood Pembroke table crossbanded in kingwood and inlaid with ebony, 29ins high. **$450 £225**

Early Regency Pembroke table in mahogany, crossbanded and inlaid with ebony. **$550 £275**

Late 18th century satinwood inlaid Pembroke table on square tapering legs. **$1,020 £510**

Small Sheraton period satinwood Pembroke table crossbanded in kingwood. **$1,755 £900**

George III decorated satinwood Pembroke table. **$2,000 £1,000**

An elegant George III mahogany Pembroke table in the French Hepplewhite style. **$4,095 £2,100**

Late 19th century
French walnut side
table on cabriole
legs with scroll feet.
**$195 £100**

Late 17th century oak
side table of faded
colour.    **$280 £140**

Late 17th century Spanish
oak side table.  **$300 £150**

Regency period brass
inlaid rosewood side
table.    **$680 £350**

Early 17th century oak
side table of good
colour.    **$500 £250**

19th century kingwood
side table in the French
style.    **$600 £300**

Late 18th century Dutch
marquetry side table.
**$850 £425**

George III gilt side
table with a marble
top.  **$1,000 £500**

An Irish Chippendale
serving table in
mahogany with a
heavily carved under-
frame in the rococo
style.  **$1,520 £780**

19th century Indian
brass folding table.
**$50 £25**

Late 19th century
Victorian beechwood
stretcher table with
ebony string inlay.
**$85 £45**

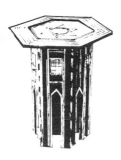

19th century inlaid
Moorish table, 14ins
high.      **$40 £20**

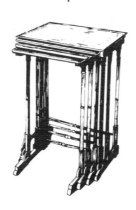

Early 19th century
mahogany centre table
with floral decoration.
**$800 £400**

19th century gilt
occasional table with
a rouge marble top.
**$400 £200**

Louis Philippe period
Gueridon table in
kingwood with ormolu
mounts and rose marble
top.      **$585 £300**

Victorian burr walnut
table on a spiral twist
column and tripod base,
1ft 8ins diameter.
**$130 £65**

George III mahogany
quarto tables, 27 ins high.
**$730 £375**

Good quality Regency
rosewood chess table
with gilt decoration.
**$280 £140**      53

# SOFA TABLES

Regency pedestal sofa table in mahogany, the edges and legs inlaid with coromandel wood.
**$960 £480**

Early 19th century mahogany sofa table with a platform base and paw feet.
**$875 £450**

A finely figured Regency rosewood sofa table, circa 1830.
**$1,080 £540**

George III mahogany sofa table with splayed legs, 59ins long when open, 35ins wide, 26ins high. **$1,950 £1,000**

Early 19th century rosewood sofa table with turned supports and splayed feet with brass castors.
**$1,140 £570**

A nice plain mahogany sofa table, circa 1800, 35ins wide, 26ins deep, 28ins high.
**$1,460 £750**

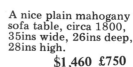

Regency rosewood sofa table on splay feet with brass claw castors. **$1,600 £800**

A superb brass inlaid rosewood sofa table.
**$1,800 £900**

Late 18th century coromandel wood sofa table crossbanded with satinwood.
**$3,410 £1,750**

Victorian mahogany teapoy on a carved tripod base. **$230 £115**

Early Victorian rosewood teapoy on a barley twist column with cabriole legs. **$250 £125**

Regency rosewood teapoy on a carved stretcher base. **$280 £140**

William IV figured walnut teapoy on a shaped platform base with paw feet. **$280 £140**

Early 19th century mahogany teapoy. **$300 £150**

A fine early Victorian rosewood teapoy inlaid with mother of pearl. **$360 £180**

A fine early 19th century rosewood teapoy. **$400 £200**

A fine Victorian papier mache teapoy inlaid with mother of pearl. **$420 £210**

Regency brass inlaid rosewood teapoy on splayed feet with brass claw castors. **$600 £300**

# TRUNKS

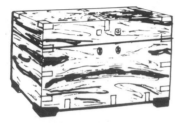

19th century camphor wood trunk with brass straps and corners. **$200 £100**

Late 18th century elm dower chest. **$150 £75**

George III panelled oak chest inlaid with fruitwood. **$320 £160**

Late 17th century oak coffer with primitive decoration, 49ins long, 20ins deep, 27½ins high. **$450 £225**

18th century oak mule chest with three drawers. **$400 £200**

17th century carved oak rug chest. **$900 £450**

16th century Gothic oak coffer of good rich patina. **$1,600 £800**

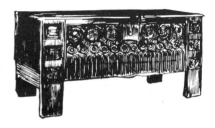

An excellent 14th century oak chest. **$12,000 £6,000**

Early 19th century mahogany linen press in two sections, 3ft 2ins wide. **$280 £140**

Victorian mahogany wardrobe with two mirror doors, 1.86m. wide.. **$90 £45**

George III serpentine fronted mahogany wardrobe on paw feet. **$400 £200**

Superb quality mahogany wardrobe of the late 18th century 4ft 3ins wide. **$500 £250**

Georgian mahogany wardrobe with finely figured oval panels to the doors. **$650 £325**

18th century mahogany clothes press, 8ft 4ins high, 5ft 9ins wide. **$600 £300**

Late 18th century French armoire in oak with steel fittings. **$840 £420**

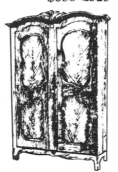

Early 19th century French walnut armoire. **$800 £400**

17th century Flemish oak armoire with a carved frieze and ebony panels, 7ft high. **$2,400 £1,200**

## WASHSTANDS

Late 19th century mahogany washstand with a tiled back and marble top.
**$70 £35**

Late 19th century walnut washstand with a white marble top.
**$50 £25**

Late Victorian walnut washstand with a figured marble top.
**$70 £35**

Late 18th century mahogany washstand.
**$200 £100**

Late 18th century mahogany washstand with a 14ins square top when closed.
**$190 £95**

A good quality George III serpentine front dressing table in satinwood.
**$480 £240**

19th century marquetry corner washstand.
**$1,000 £500**

Georgian mahogany enclosed washstand with a fitted exterior extending mirror and tambour top opening to form a dressing table, circa 1760.
**$660 £330**

An extremely fine quality chinoiserie japanned dressing table. **$5,000 £2,50**

Victorian burr walnut whatnot with shaped shelves and a fretwork gallery.  $280 £140

Victorian walnut whatnot with a brass rail.  $140 £70

Regency mahogany whatnot with brass string inlay and a pierced brass gallery. $220 £110

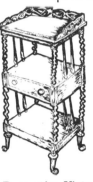

Decorative Victorian rosewood whatnot with a fretted gallery. $360 £180

19th century faded rosewood whatnot of unusual delicate design 4ft 2ins high.  $340 £170

George III mahogany whatnot 20ins wide, 18ins deep, 49ins high.  $420 £210

Late 18th century mahogany whatnot with cupboard, 58ins high, circa 1780.  $500 £250

An unusual small mahogany whatnot circa 1800.  $550 £275

An unusual George III double canterbury-whatnot in medium colour mahogany, 14ins square, 40ins high.  $700 £350

Early 19th century finely grained mahogany wine cooler on lions paw feet. $400 £200

Late 18th century octagonal cellarette on short splayed legs. $450 £225

George II mahogany wine waiter on ogee feet. $550 £275

William IV mahogany cellarette on fine turned legs. $400 £200

A fine 19th century mahogany wine cellarette, cross banded and inlaid with satinwood, holly, ebony and boxwood, on a detachable mahogany stand of a later date. $630 £315

George III mahogany domed top wine cooler with brass carrying handles. $640 £320

Late 18th century mahogany oval brass bound cellarette, complete with the original stand.
60 $1,020 £510

Fine 18th century mahogany hexagonal wine cooler with brass bindings and handles. $1,320 £660

18th century mahogany and brass bound wine cooler, on shaped legs. $2,400 £1,200

Victorian mahogany work box with drawer. **$250 £125**

Good quality early Victorian mahogany sewing table with drop flaps and a U shaped centre support. **$360 £180**

George III mahogany drop flap work table, circa 1800.
**$310 £155**

Early 19th century combined games and sewing table in rosewood. **$600 £300**

A good quality Victorian papier mache work table with floral and gilt decoration.
**$650 £325**

A fine quality Regency mahogany work table.
**$680 £340**

An unusual Regency sewing table with a rising screen and adjustable reading slope. **$960 £480**

19th century French walnut and marquetry games table with a chess board top and ormolu mounts.
**$1,000 £500**

Regency period combined games table and work table in rosewood with inlaid brass decoration.
**$1,500 £750**

61

# WRITING TABLES/BONHEUR DE JOUR

Victorian mahogany library table on turned and fluted legs. **$90 £45**

Victorian mahogany writing table on turned legs. **$80 £40**

Edwardian inlaid rosewood writing table with inset leather top. 2ft 6ins wide. **$180 £90**

19th century brass inlaid bonheur de jour in mahogany with satinwood lining. **$650 £325**

Early 18th century mahogany architect's table. **$625 £320**

Edwardian ladies writing desk with satinwood and floral panels. **$900 £450**

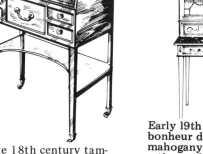

A fine red boulle bonheur de jour with ormolu embellishments, circa 1850. **$1,200 £600**

Late 18th century tambour fronted mahogany desk, 69cm. wide. **$1,860 £930**

Early 19th century bonheur de jour in mahogany with satinwood inlay. **$3,500 £1,750**

# BELLEEK

19th century Belleek lattice work basket. **$150 £75**

Belleck hot water vessel and stand 14ins high. **$310 £155**

# CHINA

A centrepiece impressed Belleek Co. Fermanagh 12.75ins high **$360 £180**

# BOW

A Bow figure of Kitty Clive **$1,200 £600**

An early Bow candlestick depicting a pheasant. **$660 £330**

Bow porcelain figure of the infant Bacchus circa 1750. **$720 £360**

# CAPO DI MONTE

A rare Royal Vienna style fairing with the Naples Capo di Monte mark. **$480 £240**

The Declaration by Giuseppe Gricci **$26,400 £13,200**

Pantaloon from the Italian comedy, modelled by Giuseppe Gricci. **$7,700 £3,850**

# CAUGHLEY

19th century blue and white Caughley jug. **$120 £60**

An early 19th century Caughley pickle dish. **$60 £30**

A Victorian Caughley jug. **$120 £60**

Rare Chelsea botanical
plate by Hans Sloane. $6,800
£3,400

Chelsea teapot and cover
by Jeffryes Hamett O'Neale.
£450    $1,260 £630

Rare Chelsea figure of a
Chinese man, 7ins high.
$17,600
£8,800

Pair of Chelsea bird
models 4¾ins high.
$4,650 £2,325

Rare Chelsea coloured
acanthus leaf cream jug.
$5,500
£2,750

Chelsea red anchor
sweetmeat dish. $1,440
£720

**CHINESE**

19th century Canton
vase 24ins tall. $110 £55

Transitional period blue
and white Chinese porcelain
stem cup.        $260 £130

K'ang Hsi blue and
white bottle.
$540 £270

18th century Chinese
goose tureen.
**64**    $15,180 £7,590 ·

K'ang Hsi period
porcelain figures.
$8,400 £4,200

T'ang dynasty figure
of a horse.
$72,000 £36,000

# COALBROOKDALE/COPELAND

Modern Coalbrookdale urn. **$300 £150**

Floral encrusted Coalbrookdale vase circa 1825. **$200 £100**

Large Copeland tazza circa 1836. **$140 £70**

## COALPORT

A Coalport jug printed in dark blue, 21.5cm. high. **$260 £130**

A fine Coalport vase and cover circa 1830. **$200 £100**

A red and gilt Coalport cup and saucer. **$24 £12**

## CREAMWARE

19th century creamware black transfer plate. **$72 £36**

Late 18th century Leeds creamware mug. **$900 £450**

Leeds creamware baluster jug. **$840 £420**

## DELFT

An early Dutch Delft pottery cow. **$700 £350**

17th century Dutch Delft tulip vase. **$1,200 £600**

Blue and white Southwark Delft mug. **$3,850 £1,925**

# CHINA
## DERBY

Small 18th century Derby putto $60 £30

Early 19th century shaped Crown Derby dish. $150 £75

Victorian Derby candlestick. $150 £75

## DOULTON

One of a pair of Doulton Lambeth vases by Florence Barlow. $340 £170

A Doulton Burslem jug and basin. $40 £20

Circular Doulton Lambeth salad bowl. $120 £60

## DRESDEN

19th century Dresden cup and saucer. $110 £55

Dresden figure of Europa and the Bull. $240 £120

Mid 19th century Dresden figure of Bacchus. £175 $480 £240

## FAIRINGS

*Returning at one o'clock in the morning*

Returning at 1 o'clock in the morning. $60 £30

*The Babes in the Wood*

The Babes in the Wood. $840 £420

80 Strokes of the Pulse. $1,080 £540

19th century shaped Imari dish. **$24 £12**

Large 19th century Imari vase, 18ins high. **$200 £100**

## JARDINIERES

Pair of 18th century Arita-Imari high shouldered jars 30ins high.
**$6,000 £3,000**

Victorian square based jardiniere and stand, circa 1880. **$300 £150**

Victorian hand painted pot and stand. **$200 £100**

## MEISSEN

French style jardiniere and stand circa 1870.
**$350 £175**

Meissen ecuelle cover and stand. **$1,510 £755**

19th century Meissen female figure. **$250 £125**
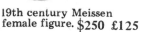

Pair of Meissen gold-finches. **$1,620 £810**

# CHINA
## MENNECY

A fine Mennecy Magot figure. $2,400 £1,200

An exceptionally fine pair of ormolu mounted Mennecy figures. $22,000 £11,000

## MINTON

An early 19th century Minton greyhound. $200 £100

One of a pair of Minton vases circa 1845, 10ins high. $600 £300

An important Minton pot pourri vase 28ins high. $2,000 £1,000

## MOORCROFT

Moorcroft pottery vase painted with fruit and foliage circa 1930. $72 £36

Pair of Moorcroft pottery mallet shaped vases circa 1920. $120 £60

Moorcroft pottery bowl decorated with chrysanthemums. $150 £75

## PARIAN

A Bailey Murrells & Co. Parian figure of Palmerston, circa 1865, 17in. high. $151 £80

Parian figure of a partially robed female. $120 £60

Victorian Parian figure 12ins high. $80 £40

68

The Shrimpers.   $50  £25

Trafalgar Square.  $100 £50

The International
Exhibition 1851.
$200  £100

St. Pauls Cathedral.
$420  £210

Sir Robert Peel.
$1,080  £540

The Matador.
$1,140  £570

**PRATTWARE**

Prattware plate 'The
Hop Queen'. $100  £50

Rare Prattware Toby
jug circa 1780. $480  £240

A small Victorian
Prattware vase.
$120  £60

**ROCKINGHAM**

A fine early Rockingham
plate.          $820  £410

Early Rockingham pot
pourri jar and cover. $820  £410

An early Rockingham pot
pourri jar and cover.
$860  £430

69

## CHINA
### RUSKIN

Ruskin eggshell pottery bowl circa 1910. $130 £65

Ruskin pottery vase, circa 1906. $110 £55

### SALTGLAZE

A fine octagonal salt-glaze plate. $560 £280

Saltglaze pottery Toby jug of Lord Nelson. $120 £60

A Ruskin shouldered pottery vase circa 1905. $84 £42

19th century saltglaze puzzle jug. $96 £48

### SEVRES

One of a pair of 19th century vases decorated with figures and landscapes 2ft 6ins high. $2,000 £1,000

One of a pair of 19th century Sevres vases. $600 £300

### SPODE

An extremely fine pair of Sevres Rose Pompadour vases. $19,800 £9,900

Small 19th century Spode dish. $30 £15

Oval Spode pearlware blue and white dish circa 1835. $36 £18

Hexagonal Spode plate with bird and feather decoration. $72 £36

One of a pair of
Victorian Staffordshire
dogs. **$60 £30**

Staffordshire childs
plate depicting Queen
Victoria. **$96 £48**

19th century figure of
Prince Albert.**$100 £50**

Staffordshire group
'Othello and Iago'.
**$580 £290**

Staffordshire figure
'The Vicar and Moses',
9½ins high. **$840 £420**

A fine Staffordshire
figure 'The Grapplers'.
**$1,740 £870**

'Marshall Marnaud',
circa 1854. **$110 £55**

# SUNDERLAND LUSTRE

19th century figure
of Byron, 7ins tall. **$60 £30**

Figure of 'The Duke
of Edinburgh'. **$72 £36**

Victorian Sunderland
Lustre jug. **$84 £42**

Sunderland Lustre
punch bowl.**$100 £50**

19th century Lustre
jug. **$40 £20**

# VICTORIAN CHINA

Florian vase made at
MacIntyres circa 1893.
$255 £125

One of a pair of
Victorian vases. $50 £25

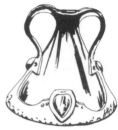

Bretby pottery vase.
$150 £75

Victorian biscuit
barrel.  $20 £10

Masons blue and white
jug and basin.  $48 £24

Victorian moustache cup.
$20 £10

## WEDGWOOD

Victorian silver mounted
biscuit barrel.  $110 £55

Wedgwood black
basalt bust. $480 £240

19th century green
Wedgwood plate. $12 £6

One of a pair of
variegated  vases circa
1780.     $2,040 £1,020

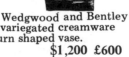

Wedgwood and Bentley
variegated creamware
urn shaped vase.
$1,200 £600

The  Wedgwood  Pegasus
vase.   $2,040 £1,020

# WORCESTER

# CHINA

A Flight Barr and Barr apple green vase. $180 £90

A Grainger Worcester sauce tureen circa 1810. $160 £80

Victorian Royal Worcester vase, 16ins high. $300 £150

18th century Worcester porcelain dish. $480 £240

Dr. Wall period hot water jug. $3,080 £1,540

An early Worcester group of two birds. $7,150 £3,575

## ENOCH WOOD

Mustard pot by Enoch Wood circa 1805. $60 £30

Bust of Napoleon by Enoch Wood. $400 £200

A fine bust of John Wesley. $200 £100

## RALPH WOOD

Rare Ralph Wood Toby jug, circa 1750. $660 $330

'St. George and Dragon' by Ralph Wood. $960 £480

Ralph Wood Planter Toby jug. $450 £225

73

A Davenport Longport dessert plate. $24 £12

A pair of Martinware lovebirds. $840 £420

Longton Hall coffee cup circa 1760. $110 £55

A pair of Frankenthal figures of harvesters, 4ins high. $960 £480

New Hall lustre cup and saucer circa 1815. $36 £1

Linthorpe vase painted with white flowers. $120 £60

Rare Victorian Swansea Coronation mug. $480 £240

A Pilkington Royal Lancastrian vase. $300 £150

A rare Wheilden figure. $300 £150

A Wrotham slipware Tyg by George Richardson. $3,960 £1,980

Wrotham pottery jug by George Richardson $3,960 £1,980

Victorian oak cased
striking bracket clock.
$70 £35

Edwardian bracket clock
in a mahogany case.
$120 £60

Late Regency bracket
clock by James McCabe.
$1,000 £500

Red walnut cased bracket
clock by H.J. Taylor
with a musical striking
movement. $1,300 £650

Ebonised case bracket
clock by John Williamson
circa 1700. $800 £400

A large early 19th
century ebonised bracket
clock with a three train
movement. $1,100 £550

Mahogany cased bracket
clock by John Gerrard.
$3,300 £1,650

A fine bracket clock by
Thomas Smith of Norwich.
$2,350 £1,175

Rare bracket clock by
Daniel Quare.
$8,000 £4,000

Small Victorian brass carriage clock with an eight day movement.
**$240 £120**

Victorian carriage clock with enamel and brass dial and fluted pillars, 13cm. high.
**$300 £150**

A French brass oval carriage clock by Drocourt, 15cm.
**$2,160 £1,080**

19th century French brass carriage clock with a cloisonne enamel centre panel surrounded by pierced and chased floral scrolls. **$600 £300**

An unusual Victorian brass carriage clock with a pale green enamel dial, ½ hour strike and alarm.
**$380 £190**

Victorian brass carriage clock with full repeating sonniere movement on two gongs.
**$610 £305**

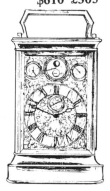

A fine quality 19th century French carriage clock by Leroy et Fils of Paris. **$1,380 £690**

An unusual French carriage clock in an ormolu case, 10ins high.
**$1,030 £515**

An exceptionally fine carriage clock by Frederick Dent.
**$28,000 £14,000**

A 19th century French clock set in ormolu with decorative porcelain plaques.   $500  £250

19th century vase shaped clock set in bleu de roi mounted with ormolu.   $840  £420

A good 18th century Sevres garniture de cheminee decorated with male and female figures in ormolu.   $960  £480

An ormolu and cloisonne enamel French striking clock with a pair of complementary ormolu and porcelain side pieces, circa 1860, 15ins high.
$1,260  £630

# GRANDFATHER CLOCKS

Late 18th century longcase clock by Waldre of Arundel, with a white enamel face and oak case.
**$270  £135**

18th century mahogany cased grandfather clock with a brass dial and dead beat escapement.
**$660  £330**

Good quality Scottish longcase clock, circa 1830.
**$660  £330**

An attractive small size ebonised longcase clock with a caddy top, brass face and eight day movement by John Wise of London, circa 1695.
**$1,680  £840**

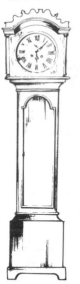

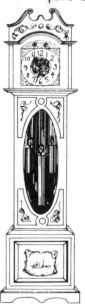

A fine Edwardian inlaid mahogany longcase clock.
**$1,560  £780**

A rare pollard oak and oyster walnut longcase clock by Thomas Ogden of Halifax, circa 1750.
**$3,000  £1,500**

A superb Edwardian chiming grandfather clock in a fine mahogany case, 9ft tall.
**$3,240  £1,620**

A fine walnut and marquetry longcase clock by Jurigthoff of Bath, 7ft 8ins tall. **$4,400  £2,200**

78

Victorian brass reproduction lantern clock with an eight day French movement. $130 £65

A good original wing lantern clock, circa 1670. $1,920 £960

Late 17th century lantern clock with verge escapement and long pendulum. $1,260 £630

## MANTEL CLOCKS

19th century walnut cased mantel clock with an American movement. $60 £30

Late 19th century French marble and spelter striking mantel clock. $100 £50

Louis XVI ormolu and marble mantel clock. $440 £220

Mid 19th century ormolu mantel clock in the French rococo style, 12ins high. $500 £250

18th century Buhl mantel clock with fine ormolu enrichments. $750 £375

Blue porcelain and ormolu clock by Aubert and Klaftenberger of Geneva, circa 1850. $850 £425

# CLOCKS
## SKELETON CLOCKS

Victorian brass skeleton clock with a half-second dead beat escapement. $380 £190

Small scroll design hour striking skeleton clock. $660 £330

An exceptionally fine skeleton clock with a two train eight day movement, 20ins high. $1,100 £550

## WALL CLOCKS

American wall clock by Jerome and Co., New Haven, Connecticut. $70 £35

Late 18th century mahogany wall clock with a 16ins dial and fusee movement. $160 £80

Regency period Parliament clock in a mounted rosewood case with brass inlay. $160 £80

19th century eight day red boulle wall clock with ormolu decoration. $480 £240

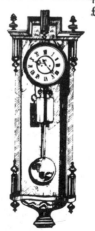

Attractive and well-figured walnut striking Vienna regulator. $440 £220

18th century Cartel clock by Fieffe, ormolu work by Cressant, 4ft 5ins high. $35,200 £17,600

# BEILBY

# GLASS

Wine Glass by William and Mary Beilby with a flared round funnel bowl, circa 1765. **$1,032 £516**

A Beilby ogee bowl wine glass, 5¼ins high. **$348 £174**

An heraldic goblet decorated by Beilby of Newcastle, 8½ins high. **$7,000 £3,500**

## BOHEMIAN

19th century Bohemian glass flask. **$132 £66**

Victorian Bohemian glass goblet. **$60 £30**

Late 18th century Bohemian double overlay beaker. **$230 £115**

## BOTTLES

Cobalt blue poison bottle. **$6 £3**

A blown and moulded sealed bottle dated 1775. **$144 £72**

A blown and moulded sealed bottle dated 1802. **$72 £36**

## BRISTOL

A fine Bristol finger bowl marked I. Jacobs. **$360 £180**

A 19th century Bristol blue ketchup bottle. **$84 £42**

An 18th century Bristol five bottle cruet. **$4,800 £2,400**  81

# GLASS
## CARNIVAL

Victorian orange
Carnival glass bowl. $12 £6

## CRANBERRY

Victorian Carnival
glass vase. $12 £6

Victorian mauve
Carnival glass bowl.
$14 £7

19th century Cranberry
glass basket with a
plated stand. $44 £22

Cranberry fluted
glass vase.
$24 £12

Victorian Cranberry
glass water jug, 10ins
high. $36 £18

Victorian Cranberry
glass four branch
epergne. $70 £35

## DECANTERS

An early 19th
century plain glass
decanter. $54 £27

Late 18th century
engraved decanter.
$84 £42

Early 18th century
cut glass decanter. $84 £42

18th century decanter
engraved 'Port'. $150
£75

A fine heavy ships
decanter, circa 1860. $180
£90

Pair of decanters with matching
wine glasses from the Prince
Regent Service. $2,600 £1,300

Late 17th century
English decanter
jug. $2,690 £1,345

82

An early cut glass boat shaped bowl. $336 £168

Glass butter dish, cover and stand, circa 1810. $90 £45

A good early English sweetmeat glass. $420 £210

An early English covered bowl. $1,070 £535

Victorian spun glass house, complete with glass dome and wooden stand, 51 cm. high. $240 £120

An early English glass ewer circa 1760. $140 £70

A small Georgian glass jug circa 1810, 4½ins high. $84 £42

A carved cameo amber glass plaque by G. Woodhall, 16.5cm. high. $3,300 £1,650

Georgian tumbler engraved with figures of Faith, Hope and Charity, 3½ins high. $108 £54

**GALLE**

A fine signed Galle vase. $324 £162

A cameo and marquetry vase by Galle with silver mounts by Cardeilhac. $2,220 £1,110

A Galle acid etched cameo vase. $480 £240

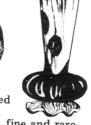

A fine and rare marquetry vase by Emile Galle, made in 1900. $5,500 £2,750 83

# GLASS
## IRISH

Irish glass yacht cream jug, circa 1800.
**$108 £54**

Pair of Irish glass boat shaped salts, circa 1800.
**$96 £48**

## KOTHGASSER, ANTON

Irish glass flat cut cream jug. **$62 £31**

Amber flash beaker by Anton Kothgasser. **$1,200 £600**

## LALIQUE

A fine amber coloured beaker signed Anton Kothgasser (1769-1851).
**$1,440 £720**

18th century amber flash beaker by Anton Kothgasser. **$900 £450**

A glass decanter by Rene Lalique 12ins high. **$480 £240**

## LOETZ

Lalique vase with a border of bacchanates.
**$3,960 £1,980**

A fine trial vase by Rene Lalique. **$432 £216**

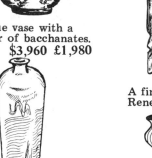

A good quality 19th century Loetz glass jug. **$204 £102**

A Loetz vase decorated with green and blue iridescence over pink. **$400 £200**

Blue and amber Loetz glass. **$624 £312**

# MARY GREGORY

Victorian 'Mary Gregory' dimpled decanter. $80 £40

A Mary Gregory cranberry glass jug 5½ins high. $68 £34

19th century Mary Gregory glass pitcher 8ins high. $60 £30

## OPAL GLASS

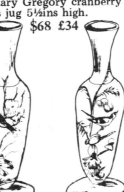

Victorian opal glass vase 10ins high. $24 £12

Pair of Victorian opal glass vases 12ins high. $40 £20

Victorian opal glass vase. $36 £18

## PAPERWEIGHTS

A St. Louis green carpet ground paperweight. $3,520 £1,760

A superb Clichy lily of the valley weight. $18,700 £9,350

A St. Louis fuchsia paperweight. $2,400 £1,200

## RAVENSCROFT

Ravenscroft crisselled decanter jug with seven vertical pincered and winged ribs, with a replaced foot. $1,500 £750

A rare Ravenscroft decanter jug of the mid 1680's. $2,400 £1,200

85

# SCENT BOTTLES

Late l9th century engraved silver scent bottle. $50 £25

Victorian green china scent bottle with a silver top. $40 £20

Mid l9th century Bohemian glass scent bottle. $96 £48

Victorian vaseline glass scent bottle. $72 £36

19th century blue and white overlay scent bottle. $84 £42

Fine double ended blue overlay scent bottle with silver tops. $84 £42

Small Victorian silver scent bottle. $50 £25

# SNUFF BOTTLES

Carved ivory snuff bottle. $140 £70

A mutton fat jade bottle carved with figures playing chequers $255 £125

Chinese carved agate snuff bottle. $280 £140

Chinese overlay snuff bottle. $312 £156

A Chinese glass snuff bottle painted on the inside with horses. $510 £252

Chinese carved agate snuff bottle. $810 £400

A white jade bottle with russet markings carved with a boy and a tiger. $2,220 £1,100

Important Chinese snuff bottle in Canton enamel with a blue Ch'ien mark, 2¼ins high. $9,000 £4,500

# STOURBRIDGE/SUNDERLAND BRIDGE    GLASS

An attractive Stourbridge inkwell decorated with millefiori design. $156 £78

Stourbridge inkwell with millefiori design. $180 £90

Sunderland Bridge engraved decanter, circa 1840. $230 £115

Sunderland Bridge rummer with a bucket bowl. $156 £78

## TANTALUS

A fine quality Victorian tantalus in an oak case with silver mounts. $216 £108

19th century plated decanter stand with three bottles. $156 £78

Fine ebony decanter suite believed to be the property of Napoleon III, circa 1850. $1,000 £500

## TIFFANY

19th century Tiffany vase in iridescent golden glass. $600 £300

Rare Tiffany scent bottle. $1,200 £600

Rare Tiffany inkwell. $1,800 £900

Tiffany amber lustre glass. $480 £240

## WEBB

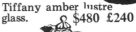

A Webb glass cameo vase, 9ins high. $504 £252

A Webb yellow and white satin glass vase. $420 £210

An exceptionally fine Webb cameo glass decanter. $1,560 £780

A balustroid vase in iridescent blue green 7¾ins high. **$84 £42**

One of an unusual pair of bubble glass, flared rim vases painted with 19th century military scenes. **$120 £60**

Victorian pink glass jug with an amber handle. **$36 £18**

A fine satin glass bottle 7½ins high. **$180 £90**

19th century cut glass and plated centrepiece. **$72 £36**

19th century milk glass crimped bowl. **$24 £12**

One of a pair of Victorian ruby glass lustres. **$100 £50**

Victorian crimson glass epergne with centre trumpet, 60cm. high overall. **$108 £54**

Victorian cut glass candlestick. **$12 £6**

18th century colour twist green and red wine glass. $96 £48

An early balustroid wine glass. $114 £57

An excise wine glass with a round funnel bowl engraved with a sprig of fruiting vine, circa 1745. $144 £72

17th century ale glass with a wrytten bowl. $192 £96

Cordial glass with a flared bucket bowl 6¾ins high, circa 1760. $192 £96

A composite wine glass with a waisted bowl set over a multiple spiral air twist section 7ins high, circa 1745. $240 £120

Ratafia glass with a narrow straight sided funnel bowl, circa 1745. $276 £138

Early 18th century mead glass. $420 £210

Lead glass goblet with a serpentine stem, circa 1685, 11½ins high. $530 £265

A baluster wine glass with a round funnel bowl 5¾ins high, circa 1710. $636 £318

Giant lead glass goblet with prunts on the stem, circa 1690, 12½ins high. $624 £312

A magnificent wine glass with a conical bowl, circa 1715. $720 £360

**89**

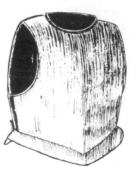

A good siege weight
pair of Cromwellian
breast and back plates.
$220 £110

A fine complete suit of
Pikemans armour, English
circa 1600, comprising
'Pot' gorget, breast,
backplate and tassels.
$1,080 £540

A good 16th century
half suit of black and
white Landsknecht
armour bearing traces
of original gold painted
decoration. $1,920 £960

A fine suit of 18th
century armour.
$1,800 £900

An extremely fine and
decorative electrotype
replica of the Louvre
Henri II embossed
armour, complete in
every detail
$2,400 £1,200

An exceptionally fine
16th century Italian
full suit of armour made
of bright steel, on a
wooden stand
$3,600 £1,800

A large Animalier group of gun dogs signed L. Bureau, 14ins high.

**$600 £300**

A large bronze of Kaiser Wilhelm I wearing full uniform and decorations, 17ins high. **$440 £220**

A bronzed brass figure of Napoleon, 7ins high.

**$130 £65**

Mene bronze of an Arab stallion, 'Ibrahim'.

**$1,200 £600**

Bronze of an African Horseman being attacked by a lion, by Isidore Bonheur. **$1,440 £720**

'Forager', a beautiful bronze of a foxhound by Adrian Jones, 10ins long. **$840 £420**

Ivory and bronze female figure by Chiparus.

**$2,860 £1,430**

Figure of a young girl with hoop by Preiss.
**$960 £480**

'Pluto and Proserpine' a large bronze after Bernini, 30½ins high.

**$8,800 £4,400**

# BUCKETS AND HODS

Victorian brass helmet coal scuttle. $50 £25

Victorian painted coal scuttle. $60 £30

Late Victorian cast iron coal box. $110 £55

Late Victorian oak coal box with brass fittings. $44 £22

18th century oval copper scuttle of unusual design. $190 £90

George III brass coal scoop. $84 £42

Victorian Fireman's leather bucket decorated with a Coat of Arms. $90 £45

18th century Dutch brass cauldron with paw feet. $170 £85

Late 18th century pierced brass log box with liner. $190 £95

A fine 18th century brass bucket. $420 £210

A brass handled and banded mahogany plate pail, circa 1755. $480 £240

A fine George III mahogany bucket with brass fittings, circa 1790. $780 £390

Large Victorian
copper jelly mould.
$60 £30

Brass chamber stick
with a drip pan.
$24 £12

Finely detailed Adam period
door knocker, 9in. high.
$64 £32

Late 18th century brass
tavern footman.$180 £90

George III copper
saucepan complete
with lid. $72 £36

Victorian copper
watering can.
$36 £18

A fine quality copper
kettle with a brass
spout. $96 £48

Four gallon copper
measure. $130 £65

19th century brass
parrot cage.
$190 £90

Early 19th century
brass revolving magazine
rack on shaped legs
with paw feet. $170 £85

19th century brass club
fender with a leather
seat. $300 £150

Early 19th century brass
fire-irons complete
with matching stand.
$96 £48

# INSTRUMENTS

Victorian brass letter scales.    $64 £32

Mid Victorian coffee grinder.    $48 £24

Victorian chromatic stereoscope. $36 £18

Victorian kitchen scales with brass pans and cast iron stand. $72 £36

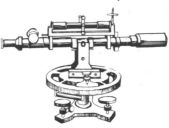

Mid 19th century brass theodolite. $400 £200

Jones improved type microscope, complete with box, circa 1800. £110    $320 £160

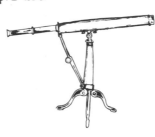

Early 19th century table telescope by Cary of London.    $340 £170

Magnificent lacquered brass 19th century pillar sextant by Cary of London.    $1,560 £780

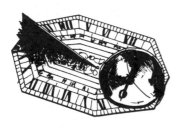

Butterfield silver pocket dial, 2.1/8ins long.
$710 £355

17th century ivory pillar dial.  $2,400 £1,200

A fine marine chronometer, circa 1770. $6,600 £3,300

Wood dyers iron
cauldron circa 1800. $84 £42

Victorian cast iron
garden seat.   $420 £210

Cast iron ships
chandlers sign.
$180 £90

Victorian iron work
plant stand. $60 £30

**LEAD**

An attractive wrought
iron garden bench.
$840 £420

A large Victorian
wrought iron urn.
$290 £145

An early lead garden
urn 2ft 5ins high. $290 £145

A good quality lead
figure of a youth in
costume playing a
violin, 4ft 1ins high.
$1,080 £540

Late 18th century lead
figure 2ft 8ins high.
$580 £290

A good late 18th
century lead figure of
a child, 3ft high. $1,100 £550

19th century lead
greyhound 2ft 7ins
high, on a Portland
stone base. $620 £310

A lead figure of
Mercury, 46ins
high. $530 £265

95

A 19th century brass carriage lamp. $80 £40

19th century brass argand lamp with white glass shades. $116 £58

Victorian brass oil lamp with a green glass shade. $104 £52

A fine Daum overlay lamp with a purple and cloudy glass ground. $600 £300

A very fine quality Muller lamp. $1,200 £600

Tiffany lamp with a gilt bronze base and coloured glass poppy pattern shade. $1,968 £984

Large Victorian copper street lamp. $96 £48

Victorian bronze ship's lantern. $180 £90

A fine Victorian copper and steel lantern with the original glass, 3ft high. $330 £165

Small 19th century Dutch brass hanging light. $150 £75

Regency twelve light brass chandelier with glass drops. $450 £225

French rococo gilt brass nine light chandelier, 35ins tall, 21ins wide. $550 £275

A fine late 18th century pewter tankard. $120 £60

18th century pewter charger with a London mark. $150 £75

18th century German pewter lidded tankard. $200 £100

Early 19th century one gallon harvest measure with scroll handle, 11½in. high. $280 £140

A pewter spoon rack by A. Heiddan, Lubeck, circa 1820. $320 £160

Charles I bun shaped covered flagon. $2,800 £1,400

18th century pewter measure. $130 £65

18th century pewter jug. $50 £25

19th century Japanese pewter Ting, 28.5cm. $80 £40

One of a pair of mid 17th century pewter candlesticks, 9½in. high. $17,000 £8,500

A large rare pewter Montieth bowl, circa 1700. $1,600 £800

Victorian pewter coffee pot. $50 £25

Embossed copper gun flask by P.Powell and Son. $70 £35

Embossed copper flask with stars, dots and acanthus. $100 £50

An unusual copper bodied two way powder flask. $100 £50

A silver mounted double horn powder flask. $140 £70

A rare embossed brass gun flask depicting entwined dolphins. $200 £100

A fine and rare copper 'Batty Peace Flask'. $200 £100

17th century German flattened horn powder flask. $200 £100

A 17th century engraved powder horn. $220 £110

A fine and rare Colt patent copper powder flask for the Walker model. $240 £120

A fine early 17th century powder flask of wood inlaid with concentric rings of staghorn, brass wire and circle of dots. $270 £135

17th century style powder flask with a cloth covered wood body encased in fretted iron. $360 £180

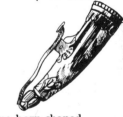

A fine horn shaped priming flask with a silver cap. $420 £210

An attractive early 19th century iron tsuba inlaid with gold, silver and Shakudo details. **$100 £50**

An attractive Japanese tsuba Shakudo Nanako with a gilt rim and flowers in high relief. **$110 £55**

Japanese iron tsuba depicting shells in high relief within a gold damascene rim. **$150 £75**

Japanese pierced iron tsuba depicting a Ho Ho bird perched in the bough of a tree. **$240 £120**

A brass tsuba of square form depicting a locust devouring foliage. **$255 £125**

Japanese pierced iron tsuba depicting Aoi leaves, flowers and tendrils **$280 £140**

An unusual tsuba of Mokko form depicting dragon flies, chrysanthemums, foliage and a fence. **$405 £200**

Shakudo tsuba carved and inlaid with bamboo trees and foliage, signed. **$500 £250**

A good brass tsuba depicting a tiger in relief being pushed by a boy in high relief, signed. **$605 £300**

A good pierced brass tsuba depicting an eagle perched on cherry tree boughs. **$705 £350**

A fine and desirable iron tsuba of squared form depicting an old effeminate Sennin. **$810 £400**

A good brass tsuba of Mokko form depicting vegetation in relief. **$810 £400**

# SILVER BASKETS

Good quality Victorian cake basket, 32ozs.. $250 £125

Small 19th century plated sugar basket. $36 £18

Victorian silver sugar basket with a blue glass liner, London 1846, 5ozs. $156 £78

Late 18th century Adam style boat shaped sugar basket. $480 £240

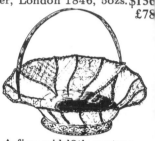

George III silver cake basket. $360 £180

## BOWLS

A fine mid 18th century basket with a cast silver rim. $580 £290

Small Victorian silver bowl, 1870, 6½ozs. $68 £34

George III pedestal bowl by Richard Cooke, 58ozs, hallmarked 1805. $2,530 £1,265

Silver wine taster. $110 £5

George III vase shaped basin by John Crouch, London 1816, 18ozs. $160 £80

A Montieth bowl by William Spachman, 1717, 73ozs. $5,720 £2,860

Charles II two-handled porringer and cover, 6in. high, 1661, 20oz. $3,900 £2,000

## BRANDY WARMERS

George III brandy warmer of good proportions. $500 £250

Victorian plated brandy warmer. $60 £30

Early George II large brandy saucepan by William Darker. $600 £300

Plain silver caddy spoon, circa 1812. $44 £22

A fluted caddy spoon dated 1814. $60 £30

Round bowl caddy spoon by Joseph Taylor 1807. $70 £35

Thistle cap caddy spoon. $72 £36

Late 18th century bright cut caddy spoon. $70 £35

Silver gilt harlequin caddy spoon, London 1845. $160 £80

Jockey cap caddy spoon circa 1798. $200 £100

## CANDELABRUM

A four light candelabrum by Emes and Barnard, 1828. $1,020 £510

One of a pair of Victorian silver gilt, seven light candelabrum. $4,180 £2,090

An impressive nine light centrepiece by Paul Storr, 1830. $5,720 £2,860

## CANDLESTICKS

A Victorian silver plated candlestick, 14ins high. $80 £40 pair

Pair of candlesticks by Benjamin Smith 52ozs 1836. $1,000 £500 pair

Pair of candlesticks by Thomas Farrer 1723 29ozs. $2,400 £1,200 pair

One of a set of four rare Louis XIV silver candlesticks by Pierre Masse of Paris, circa 1680, 7¾ins high, 88ozs. $33,000 £16,500

101

# SILVER CASTERS

Early 19th century egg shaped silver pepper caster. $240 £120

Victorian sugar caster. $340 £170

Early 18th century silver pepper caster. $760 £380

Charles II silver sugar caster of 1683, 7½ins high. $4,600 £2,300

## CHAMBERSTICKS

19th century plated chamberstick $44 £22

Silver chamberstick by Henry Wilkinson of Sheffield, 1839. $360 £180

George III chamberstick by Hannon and Crouch, London 1791 $380 £190

Silver chamberstick by Emes and Barnard 1822. $650 £325

An unusual double chamber candlestick by John Schofield, 1787 $670 £335

Silver chamberstick by John Carter, 1770. $540 £270

## COASTERS

Plain round silver coaster, 1815. $110 £55

Coaster by Peter and Anne Bateman. $280 £140

Bright cut coaster, circa 1777. $200 £100

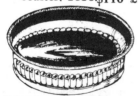

Pair of coasters by John Roberts 1808. $300 £150

Superb early 19th century tall sided silver coaster with London marks. $420 £210

One of a pair of cast vine coasters, 1810. $820 £410

102

# COFFEE POTS

Baluster coffee pot
by B. Smith, London
1840, 8½in. high.
21oz.8dwt $920 £460

19th century plated
coffee pot. $36 £18

Queen Anne coffee pot by
Anthony Nelme 1711 $2,400
£1,200

Queen Anne silver
chocolate pot.
$2,600 £1,300

Unusual Philadelphia
coffee pot by Dubois,
circa 1770, 50ozs. $5,830
£2,915

Silver coffee pot by Thomas
Williamson 1739 39ozs. $6,160
£3,080

## CRUETS

Victorian plated cruet
stand complete with six
cut glass bottles. $60 £30

George III silver egg
cruet. $310 £155

Set of three casters by
Samuel Wood 1845.
$1,620
£810

## CUPS AND BEAKERS

Silver gilt and enamel
beaker, Birmingham
1890, 19ozs. $120 £60

Fine quality silver
goblet by John
Agnell, circa 1819.
$200 £100

A fine 18th century
Swedish beaker with
delicate embossing.
$1,390 £695

Charles II silver
beaker 1678
9¾ozs.
$4,600 £2,300

## SILVER ENTREE DISHES

A fine silver entree dish and cover by Thomas Blagdon Sheffield 1830. $560 £280

10½ins rectangular Mappin and Webb entree dish. $40 £20

A fine silver entree dish by Paul Storr, 66ozs. $1,200 £600

## FLATWARE

Victorian silver christening set dated 1840. $36 £18

Silver gravy spoon by Thos. Dealy, 1806. $54 £27

Early Victorian silver marrow scoop. $92 £46

Georgian cast silver mote spoon. $84 £42

George III apple corer, London 1808, 5ins long. $150 £75

Silver gilt sifter spoon, London 1872. $74 £38

Unusual Victorian caster oil spoon, London 1842, maker E.E. $360 £180

A fine example of a Lion Sejant spoon, 1548. $960 £480

## INKSTANDS

Rare silver travellers inkwell marked H.D., London. $320 £160

George IV silver inkstand. $380 £190

19th century silver and horses hoof inkwell. $72 £36

Helmet cream jug by Charles Houghton 1786. **$160 £80**

Silver cream jug by William King of London, 1768. **$200 £100**

Excellent silver cream jug, maker A.N.S., 1767. **$250 £125**

George III silver coffee jug by Charles Wright London, 1780. **$1,050 £525**

Silver jug by Hunt and Roskill, 1872, 6½ins high. **$1,300 £650**

A fine Hester Bateman hot water jug, 1783. **$2,400 £1,200**

## KETTLES

A fine Edwardian silver spirit kettle. **$400 £200**

Part of a five piece tea and coffee set complete with tray by Barnard, 1892/94, 110ozs, the tray 117ozs. **$860 £430**

A tea kettle with spirit stand and burner by John Schofield, London 1790, 52ozs. **$700 £350**

## LADLES

Late 18th century silver punch ladle. **$116 £58**

Early 19th century silver ladle by Peter and William Bateman. **$100 £50**

Silver soup ladle, 14½ins long, 1789. **$280 £140**

Silver ladle by Robert Garrard, 1856. **$480 £240**

## SILVER MISCELLANEOUS

A seven bar toast rack on four ball feet, London 1816, 15½ozs. **$250 £125**

Silver orange strainer, circa 1765. **$180 £90**

Rare silver 'Wax Jack', London circa 1750.
**$780 £390**

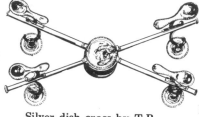

Silver dish cross by T.B. and A.H. 1780-1781.
**$660 £330**

Pierced and chased circular silver table bell. **$50 £25**

Combined fruit knife and fork Sheffield 1912.
**$30 £15**

## MUGS

An unusual glass and silver mug by John Foligno, 1855. **$200 £100**

An unusual mug by Emes and Barnard, 1815. **$170 £85**

Victorian christening mug by Elkington and Co. London 1891, engraved with the Royal Garter, 4ins high, 8.6 ozs. **$300 £150**

Silver mug by William Bateman London 1818.
**$420 £210**

'Plain Charles II pear-shaped mug by Ralph Walley (Chester 1690-2).
**$6,380 £3,190**

One of a set of four plain cylindrical mugs by De Lamerie, 1746.
**$14,960 £7,480**

Victorian silver mustard pot with a blue glass liner. **$90 £45**

Fine Victorian mustard pot by John Hunt, 1859. **$130 £65**

George IV mustard pot with a blue glass liner, London. **$220 £110**

## SALTS

George III silver salt with a gilt interior. **$72 £36**

An early Victorian silver salt cellar with a blue glass liner circa 1840. **$50 £25**

Heavy quality George III silver salt. **$110 £55**

One of a pair of small attractive silver salts by Hilliard and Thomason, 1870. **$110 £55**

One of a pair of Victorian peppers in the form of helmets with opening visors, Birmingham 1869. **$290 £145**

Fine salt cellar by Paul Storr circa 1810. **$820 £410**

## SAUCEBOATS

George II sauceboat by Thomas Farrer, circa 1730. **$430 £215**

A good quality late 18th century silver sauceboat. **$560 £280**

One of a pair of early 19th century silver sauceboats. **$900 £450**

George II sauceboat by A.F., London 1767. 7¾ins long, 11.7 ozs. **$620 £310**

George III silver sauceboat. **$650 £325**

One of a pair of George II oval double lipped sauceboats by Thomas Farrer, 1727. **$3,760 £1,980**

# SILVER
## SCISSORS AND TONGS

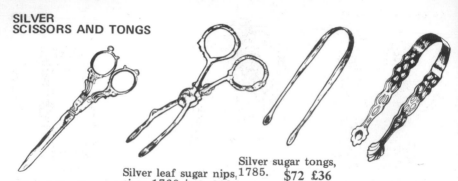

Silver leaf sugar nips, circa 1760. $60 £30

Silver sugar tongs, 1785. $72 £36

Pair of Continental silver scissors. $30 £15

Fine pair of George III cast silver sugar tongs. $110 £55

## SNUFF BOXES

Victorian silver snuff box dated 1843. $84 £42

William IV snuff box in the form of a book, London 1836. $170 £85

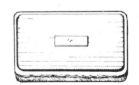

A fine Victorian silver snuff box. $230 £115

Silver gilt snuff box by Nathaniel Mills, Birmingham 1834. $600 £300

French gold snuff box with a chased floral border. $770 £385

Fine silver snuff box by T.S., Birmingham 1830. $1,020 £510

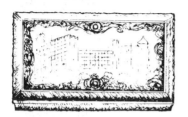

Good quality snuff box by N. Mills, 1838. $1,200 £600

An English blue glass enamelled snuff box made in the 1760's 2¼ins wide. $1,560 £780

An octagonal tortoiseshell snuff box, set with gold, jewels and enamel, 3ins wide. $3,000 £1,500

A copper based silver tankard made by Langlands and Robertson, Newcastle, 1780. $790 £395

George I tapering cylindrical tankard by Thomas Bamford, circa 1716. $1,220 £610

George II lidded quart tankard by Shaw and Priest, London 1753, 8ins high, 25½ozs. $1,680 £840

George I Scottish tankard by William Ged, Edinburgh 1715, $3,460 £1,730

Silver gilt tankard, makers mark I.B. with a rosette below, 1602, 20.3 cm high, 19ozs 17dwt. $5,170 £2,585

One of a pair of late 17th century flagons by 'Master of the Goose in a Dotted Circle' dated 1687 and 1690. $17,160 £8,580

## TEA CADDIES

One of a pair of Sheffield plate tea caddies. $110 £55

Silver tea caddy by John Newton 1736, London. $260 £130

Silver tea canister by Joseph Fainell 1720. $780 £390

Early George III engraved silver tea caddy. $720 £360

Fine quality silver tea caddy by I.P.G. 1762. $740 £370

Silver box and cover by Ebenezer Rowe, 1711, London, 8ozs 15dwt, 15cm high. $3,740 £1,870 **109**

# SILVER TEA POTS

Victorian plated teapot.
**$24 £12**

Late 19th century silver teapot, 16ozs. **$130 £65**

Silver teapot by Elizabeth and James Bland, London 1798. **$410 £205**

Teapot by Christopher Dresser with the London mark for 1880 and marked Ch. Dresser on the body. **$1,920 £960**

An important George III teapot by Hester Bateman, London 1785, 13ozs. **$720 £360**

Louis XV pear shaped teapot weighing 900 grams probably by Toulouse 1730. **$6,000 £3,000**

## TEA SETS

Small silver tea set, London 1937, 26¾ozs. **$180 £90**

A three piece Georgian semi fluted tea set by Thomas Jenkinson of London 1812, 42 ozs. **$580 £290**

Three piece tea service by Paul Storr 1813 and 1818, gross weight 61ozs 15dwt. **$1,680 £840**

110

George I spoon tray by Edward Vincent, 1717.  **$780 £390**

Victorian plated gallery tray.  **$70 £35**

Edwardian gallery tray, 27ozs.  **$200 £100**

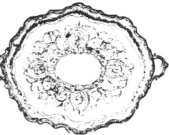

George III plain crested salver made by Robert Salmon, London 1791, 12ozs.  **$470 £235**

George III salver, London 1796.  **$530 £265**

A Victorian oval two handled tray by W & . G Sissons, Sheffield 1858, overall width 38ins.  **$1,490 £745**

## TUREENS

William IV (1832) silver tureen by Robert Garrard.  **$1,390 £695**

Good quality early 19th century plated soup tureen supported on claw feet.  **$120 £60**

Tureen and cover by John Parker and Edward Wakelin, London 1768. **$3,600 £1,800**

## URNS

19th century plated urn.  **$120 £60**

Sheffield plate urn with a gadroon and shell border.  **$470 £235**

George III silver tea urn of Neo-Classical form, London, 1789, 23½ins high.  **$960 £480**

## SILVER VASES

Victorian silver vase dated 1860, 6ozs.
$48 £24

A fine Art Nouveau silver vase. $72 £36

Mid Victorian silver vase. $40 £20

Cymric silver vase by Archibald Knox marked Birmingham 1802, 8½ins high. $760 £380

## VINAIGRETTES

Early 19th century vinaigrette. $144 £72

19th century vinaigrette by Nathaniel Mills 1832.   £60
$180 £90

Victorian silver vinaigrette with good marks. $130 £65

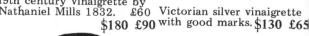

An attractive Continental silver scent flask in the form of a violin. $144 £72

Victorian silver gilt pomander with the original green leather case, London 1862, maker T.J., 2¼ins long.        $144 £72

Continental silver articulated fish.        $130 £65

## WINE COOLERS

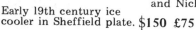

Early 19th century ice cooler in Sheffield plate. $150 £75

One of a pair of plated wine coolers by Gainsford and Nicholson. $530 £265

A fine quality George IV silver wine cooler.
$900 £450

Late 19th century carved oak banjo barometer. $72 £36

Late 18th century inlaid mahogany banjo barometer. $160 £80

Late 18th century mahogany cased barometer with satinwood inlay and crossbanding. $240 £120

18th century banjo barometer with swan necked pediment. $320 £160

George III period stick barometer by Couti. $340 £170

Fine quality large 19th century mahogany carved banjo barometer with clock. $720 £360

An exceptionally fine quality gilt framed barometer. $760 £380

George I barometer by J.N.D. Halifax of Barnsley, 1694 - 1750. $5,500 £2,750

# BOXES AND CADDIES

Victorian walnut veneered writer's companion. $50 £25

Victorian writing cabinet with brass mounts. $60 £30

19th century tortoiseshell tea caddy. $84 £42

Good quality Regency brass inlaid writing box. $170 £85

Early Victorian tortoiseshell tea caddy. $130 £65

Rare Adam satinwood and marquetry octagonal tea caddy. $170 £85

A George II mahogany table bureau with tambour top. $240 £120

Late 18th century mahogany knife box inlaid with satinwood. $500 £250

An unusual Victorian papier mache and decorated writing cabinet. $360 £180

18th century satinwood rectangular casket with inlaid panels. $370 £185

A superb 19th century burr walnut specimen box. $430 £215

An extremely fine Victorian compendium of games. $660 £330

A large, 19th century, carved wood figure of an elephant.
**$110 £55**

16th century carved wood heraldic beast.
**$340 £170**

An attractive 18th century carved limewood figure of an angel.
**$540 £270**

A fine carved wood Balinese Kris holder.
**$740 £370**

A painted Madonna and Child signed Karl Craffonaro.
**$900 £450**

15th century Italian carved wood figure of Christ.
**$1,920 £960**

A vigorously carved Napoleonic ships figurehead circa 1805.
**$3,000 £1,500**

A South German carved figure of the Archangel Gabriel.
**$4,320 £2,160**

New Zealand Maori wooden head with elaborate tattoo marks, 23.5cm high.
**$24,000 £12,000**

# DOLLS AND TOYS

Edwardian dolls house with intricate Victorian furnishings. $430 £215

Victorian toy theatre showing a sewing class in progress. $600 £300

German doll made by Herm. Steiner (1912) 16in. high. $90 £45

A good quality French doll with a porcelain head marked 'Depose tete Jumeau', 21ins high. $370 £185

Poured wax doll stamped Frederic Aldis, 20in. high. $430 £215

A wind up Victorian toy complete with original box. $240 £120

A Lehmann's clockwork 'Also' car, circa 1930, 4in. long. $96 £48

Small Victorian doll's house with a hinged front, 14ins high. $220 £110

## GLOBES

A Smiths celestial globe, circa 1840. $430 £215

An important celestial globe by Cary, dated 1790, 52ins high. $1,320 £660

One of a pair of globes by Vincenzo Coronelli circa 1690. $15,000 £7,500

Four case inro with a polished black lacquer ground. $540 £270

Four case inro decorated with a peony flower. $1,080 £540

Five case inro decorated with chrysanthemum blooms. $780 £390

A rare three case inro signed Jokasai and Yosei. $3,850 £1,925

**IVORY**

Small 19th century ivory group. $24 £12

Japanese carved ivory group of a woman carrying baskets and gourds, with a boy at her feet. $405 £200

Early 19th century carved ivory jug in the German Renaissance style. $555 £275

An unusual Oriental ivory carving 32ins long. $555 £275

17th century Spanish ivory figure of Christ. $1,575 £780

A Louis XVI ormolu mounted ivory vase by Pierre Bouthlore. $10,000 £5,000

**JADE**

A white jade figure of a bird with lotus sprays in its beak. $1,000 £500

18th century recumbent Chimera in burnt jade. $1,010 £500

An important pale green jade vase with delicate waved rims, 12ins high. $7,000 £3,500

117

## MARBLE

19th century cream marble bust of a young girl, 16ins high, signed Christopher Vicari. **$300 £150**

A fine Victorian marble figure of a child, 2ft 6ins high. **$350 £175**

A 17th century Italian Istrian marble jardiniere and stand. **$420 £210**

19th century Carrara marble bust of Admiral Nelson, 27ins high. **$750 £375**

Marble bust of Inigo Jones attributed to J.M. Rysbrack, 20½ins high. **$1,080 £540**

Roman third century marble bust of a Priest of Serapis or Helios, 75.9cm high. **$17,000 £8,500**

## MINERALS

A mass of Rhodochrosite. **$190 £95**

A well formed specimen of Hematite. **$340 £170**

A sawn and polished Geodes. **$240 £120**

Large group of clear quartz crystals. **$1,200 £600**

An iron meteorite from Arizona. **$1,440 £720**

An attractive specimen of Galena. **$360 £180**

Victorian swing mirror with barley twist supports. **$30 £15**

Late 18th century mahogany toilet mirror. **$230 £115**

18th century lacquered dressing table mirror with a fitted compartment below. **$340 £170**

Victorian gilded mirror with gesso ornamentation. **$120 £60**

Regency period convex mirror with the original gold leaf, circa 1820, 35ins high. **$180 £90**

Mid 18th century mahogany fret mirror with carved and gilded Ho Ho bird, circa 1760. **$300 £150**

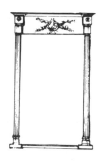

Adam style gilt Pier glass circa 1785. **$480 £240**

Carved giltwood mirror in the Chinese Chippendale style. **$1,900 £950**

George I hanging mirror in a walnut frame with carved giltwood borders. **$3,000 £1,500**

119

## MODELS

A Victorian coal fired model steam engine, 13½ins high. $200 £100

Scale model of a Waullis and Steevens 'Simplicity Roller', made in the late 20's. $2,400 £1,200

Scale model of a pony trap with original coach painted woodwork, circa 1830. $300 £150

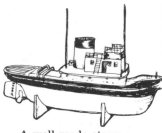

A well made steam powered model Thames tug, 58ins long. $480 £240

An 18th century Malayan deck cannon Lantaka. $200 £100

## MUSICAL BOXES

Pixie Grippa portable gramophone. $30 £15

Victorian polyphone with eight 10inch discs. $380 £190

Small oblong musical box with singing bird. $600 £300

An early 19th century singing bird in a brass cage. $620 £310

A fine First World War Edison Bell phonograph complete with cylinder records. $720 £360

19th century Swiss musical box in a rosewood case. $960 £480

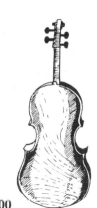

Early 19th century Dutch harp by Edward Lights. $660 £330

French harp by Renault of Paris, circa 1775. $600 £300

A gold mounted ivory concert flute by Thomas Stanesby Junior, 1740. $8,800 £4,400

19th century cello by Jules Remy of Paris. $1,080 £540

## NETSUKE

Ivory netsuke of an old woman with a large hat. $80 £40

Boxwood netsuke of a blind man squatting behind a man. $160 £80

Large netsuke in the form of a man and wife entertaining two children. $305 £150

18th century ivory netsuke of a tiger with its cub. $1,820 £900

Early 19th century netsuke representing 'contentment' sprawled on the back of a huge Fugu fish, Osaka school. $355 £175

Netsuke in the form of a peony flower signed by Masanao of Kyoto, 18th century Japanese. $4,040 £2,000

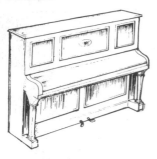

Edwardian inlaid mahogany piano.
**$80 £40**

Regency upright grand piano by Broadwoods of London. **$540 £270**

An exceptionally fine late 19th century Erard grand piano.
**$13,200 £6,600**

Rare George III mahogany Conductor's piano.
**$1,440 £720**

An Asherburg boudoir grand pianoforte, 7 octave, in a rosewood and marquetry case, 203cm. long. **$1,440 £720**

Louis XV style tulipwood salon piano. **$5,720 £2,860**

# SIGNS

An engraved brass Lloyds Insurance Agency sign. **$90 £45**

Welsh primitive shop sign of a girl in a red dress, 36ins high, circa 1830. **$500 £250**

Old English Tavern sign 'Long John Silver', 49ins high, 38ins wide. **$190 £95**

Armour bright polished Unicorn in cast iron, 24ins wide, circa 1830. **$110 £55**

An attractive old English Fishmonger's hanging shop sign, 30ins x 16ins.
**$160 £80**

19th century carved stone garden table.
$360 £180

A carved stone bench with dolphin supports, 4ft 11ins wide.
$480 £240

George III carved stone vase 24ins high.
$200 £100

A carved stone pedestal surmounted by a bronze armillary sundial, 5ft 10ins high. $900 £450

A small carved stone fountain of baroque design, 4ft high.
$800 £400

Late 18th century carved stone sundial, 4ft high.
$660 £330

## STUFFED ANIMALS

A pair of squirrels under a glass dome.
$48 £24

A mounted fox head inscribed 'Wexford Hounds 14th Oct 1904'.  $30 £15

Victorian stuffed parrot under a glass dome. $60 £30

Semi fossilised egg from an Aepyornis.
$2,800 £1,400

A cased specimen of a cockerel 'Preserved by John Pear, All Saints Green, Norwich'.
$80 £40

An extremely rare stuffed specimen of the Great Auk.  $24,000 £12,000

# TRANSPORT

Victorian wicker work bath chair with iron wheels and brass fittings. $220 £110

19th century Penny Farthing bicycle in working order. $400 £200

Dolls pram with the original upholstery in black, circa 1860, 24ins high. $110 £55

A fine mid 19th century knifegrinder's cart painted in blue and orange. $240 £120

An exceptionally fine quality mid 18th century carved and painted Norwegian sledge. $1,600 £800

Mid 19th century goat and dog cart for a child. $400 £200

19th century square shaped Brougham coach. $1,500 £750

A fine rare Showmans van. $2,000 £1,000

# UNIFORMS

A fine Officer's Lancer Tunic of the Lancashire Yeomanry. $130 £65

A good complete uniform for an Officer of the 21st Lancers. $600 £300

A fine Georgian Officer's long tailed scarlet coatee of the South East Hants Local Militia. $300 £150

# INDEX